HOW TO DEVEL

HOW TO DEVELOP YOUR ESP

A programme to help you realize your full psychic
potential

Zak Martin

Aquarian/Thorsons
An Imprint of HarperCollins*Publishers*

The Aquarian Press
An Imprint of HarperCollins*Publishers*
77–85 Fulham Palace Road,
Hammersmith, London W6 8JB
1160 Battery Street
San Francisco, California 94111–1213

Published by Aquarian 1986
7 9 10 8

A catalogue record for this book
is available from the British Library

ISBN 0 85030 488 1

Printed in Great Britain by
HarperCollinsManufacturing Glasgow

CONTENTS

For Niamh

INTRODUCTION

You are sitting at home relaxing when, for no apparent reason, you suddenly think of an old friend whom you have not seen or heard from in a long while. Five minutes later, the bell rings and your friend is standing on the doorstep ...

You visit a place for the first time and you are immediately struck by a strange sense of recognition – a feeling of 'I have been here before ...'

The telephone rings, and in the instant you lift the receiver, you know, with absolute certainty, the identity of the caller ...

You are out walking with a friend when, suddenly, you both begin to hum the same tune, in the same key, at precisely the same moment ...

Such experiences of spontaneous ESP are familiar to most people; and for individuals with a high aptitude for psychic perception, flashes of this kind are regular occurrences that may come many times in a day. However, these striking examples of the phenomenon represent only the tip of the psychic iceberg. ESP takes place *constantly* at a subliminal level, acting as a kind of invisible personal radar that scans the environment for potential danger. It is only on those occasions when the information psychically gleaned is of an unusual or dramatic nature that we become aware of the process. For example, you would not think it very extraordinary if a member of your own family arrived home shortly after you had been thinking of them: it is only when the person concerned is someone you did not expect to see that the 'coincidence' is most striking. Similarly, you would not find anything remarkable about a feeling of recognition while visiting a place that you had been to on a number of occasions.

Most of our actions are fairly routine, so that it is difficult to observe the level of ESP that accompanies them. It is when the circumstances are out of the ordinary – a visit from a long-lost friend, a serious accident, an unexpected phone call, a visit to a strange place – that the psychic factor is revealed.

Nor are our ESP impressions always recognized for what they are. Often they are rationalized as imagination or coincidence; and it is surprising how many professed sceptics of psychic matters are happy to 'explain' the phenomenon in terms of instinct and intuition.

ESP is with us all the time, and it affects our lives to a much greater extent than most people realize, and in ways that are seldom suspected. In addition to the obvious manifestations such as those already mentioned, ESP is often an important factor in matters of health, creativity, 'luck' and personal relationships. Sexual attraction, or charisma, frequently has more to do with the psychic than the physical.

These connections will become clear as you begin to understand the nature of the phenomenon.

ESP is a natural ability, present to some degree in everyone and capable of being developed with proper training; and, as with every other talent, individuals differ in their capacity for it.

This book is intended as a safe and practical guide to ESP development. The techniques included are based on my personal experience and research in this field, and on the results of many thousands of tests and experiments that I have taken part in, or conducted, during the past twenty years. If you follow the advice given and carry out the prescribed exercises regularly, you will be rewarded with increased ESP awareness and, ultimately, you will realize your full psychic potential.

Every day I receive letters from individuals who believe that they possess a strong aptitude for ESP, and claim that they would like to study the subject further and perhaps develop their psychic faculties. They invariably go on to describe their experiences at length and in great detail, recounting such events as precognitive dreams, out-of-the-body travel, *déja vu*, ghostly visitations and so on. These experiences are usually related with great enthusiasm. Sometimes my correspondents end their letters by asking for my opinion or advice on how to pursue their interest. More often, however, they are content to simply describe these experiences, and clearly they are far more interested in talking about their psychic encounters than actually doing anything positive to develop their suprasensory powers. Unfortunately, the same is true with regard to many of the societies and organizations allegedly devoted to psychic study and investigation. When it comes to psychic matters, I have found, there is often a strong element of romance and wishful thinking, and many of those involved in this field are more attracted to the *idea* of psychic power than they are interested in the practical aspects of paranormal ability.

Everyone accepts that if you want to acquire a skill or develop a particular talent – whether it is learning to drive a car or play a musical instrument – it is necessary to devote a certain amount of time and effort to the task, and that, without practice and experimentation, you cannot hope to make much progress. Where psychic training is concerned, however, it is common for many individuals to expect to be able to increase their powers of ESP merely by reading a few books on the subject. It is as though they expect to receive some kind of psychic revelation or mystical awakening just because they have acquired a little knowledge of the subject.

Despite the claims made in some magazine advertisements, there are no 'secret words of power' that will release your latent ESP abilities (or if there are, I do not know them). There is no 'key', as such, that will instantly unlock the mysteries of the mind and give you access to tremendous psychic power. Certain Kundalini yoga exercises are said to elicit ESP as a side-effect, but I have never found any evidence to support this.

Like most other things in life that are worthwhile, psychic development requires hard work and dedication. And ESP, in common with any other talent or ability, improves with practice. The more you put into this development programme, the more you can expect to get out of it.

CHAPTER ONE

PREPARATION

It is important, when embarking on any new project, to be aware of the possible pitfalls and to be properly equipped for eventualities. You may already have been warned, by well-meaning friends, about the 'terrible dangers' of becoming involved in 'the occult' or in psychic matters. Obviously, since you are reading this book, you have not been particularly impressed by such warnings, or, if you do take them seriously, you feel confident that you will be able to handle any situation that is likely to arise. I want to advise you, however, against being *too* complacent. There *are* dangers involved in psychic training, though they are not of the kind that most people might imagine. Problems can arise, not from earthbound spirits or unleashed demons, but from the developing psychic's inability to come to terms with new perspectives and new modes of perception.

Put another way, highly developed ESP is a trip that not everyone can handle. When your psychic faculties begin to emerge, your life may be changed in a profound way, leading to a shift in your perception of, and the way in which you respond to, the world around you. This change may occur instantaneously – an experience that is disconcerting to all but the most level-headed. It is much more likely, however, to be a gradual process, taking place over a period of weeks, months or even years. Either way, the results can be dramatic, and you must be ready to cope with the negative aspects of psychic development if and when they arise.

Consider, for example, the problems that can occur in relation to premonitions, which can be very upsetting for some individuals, particularly as – for reasons I will explain later – these are mostly concerned with negative or destructive events such as earthquakes, plane crashes, drownings and so on. You should be prepared for the possibility of experiencing frequent, and perhaps vivid, psychic impressions of this kind – which may occasionally involve your friends or members of your family.

Precognition has its own special problems. There is the question of whether or not you should try to warn someone if you have a premonition that something bad is about to happen to them. Unfortunately, it is not always possible – or advisable – to do so. For instance, you may have a strong impression that a certain person will be involved in a car crash, but your premonition may not be specific or detailed enough to pinpoint how or when this accident will occur. The individual concerned is unlikely to thank you for such a vague warning, since there is very little they can do to prevent your premonition from coming true. They can hardly be expected to avoid travelling in cars indefinitely – particularly as the possibility always exists that you may be wrong.

Very often, premonitions are even more vague than the one described above, and may amount to nothing more than a strong, but undefined feeling that something extremely unpleasant is about to befall a particular individual. Since the nature of the impending disaster is not known, no warning is possible.

Another problem connected with precognition is the fact that, whilst many people are fascinated by this phenomenon, many are also frightened by it. Visitors to my home in Ireland were usually impressed when I, as a child of nine or ten, was able to tell them things about themselves that I had no way of knowing – including future events. It was just a game to me at the time, but years later several of these people admitted to me that they had always been terrified that I might tell them something they didn't want to hear (which, I'm afraid, I did on more than one occasion: children are not noted for being tactful).

It is all too easy for someone who is involved in the paranormal on a daily basis to forget the tremendous fear that many people have for this subject.

Another thing you should remember is that individuals who foretell disaster are often considered to be in some way responsible when their predictions come true. In the past, witches and soothsayers have been hanged or burned at the stake for correctly prophesying poor harvests, epidemics, droughts and so on. It is an illogical but still very common reaction, of which I have personal experience. When I first began to use my abilities to help the police with unsolved cases, there was always a point – if my impressions were turning out to be correct – when the police would begin to suspect *me* of having something to do with the crime. Other psychics have actually been arrested when they were able to provide information that only the criminal could have known.

Before leaving the subject of premonitions, there is something else that I would like to point out with regard to the question of whether or not you should try to warn people when you have a strong impression that something unpleasant is about to happen. If you *do* warn them, and you *do* succeed in averting whatever disaster was about to befall, the people concerned are likely to think that you are talking nonsense – because nothing happens. *It is only when you fail to prevent such an occurrence that you are given the dubious credit of being right.*

You may find that your psychic powers work best in the area of healing – in which case you may expect to 'pick up' the symptoms (though rarely the disease itself) of the illness you are treating. And if it becomes widely known that you have abilities as a healer, people will come to you and expect you to help them with their often very complex problems and illnesses. Complete strangers will telephone you at all hours of the day and night, imploring you to do something to alleviate their suffering.

Most full-time healers derive tremendous job-satisfaction from their work. But it is an occupation that can bring you into contact with a side of life that is extremely sad and depressing and certainly not for the faint of heart.

Another disadvantage associated with increased ESP is acute sensitivity to weather conditions. Sensitivity to subtle psychic energies is accompanied by an equally delicate reaction to prevailing magnetic and cosmic conditions — including barometric pressure and the ratio of electrically charged particles in the air. In general, the more psychically attuned you become, the more easily will you be affected by weather conditions.

These are some of the disadvantages of increased ESP ability. They are greatly outweighed, of course, by the tremendous benefits that come with psychic attunement. The ability to transcend the normal sensory channels and project one's consciousness to remote locations in time and space is well worth the efforts involved in a psychic training programme such as this one. The power to tune in to people, places and events, whether past, present or future, brings with it a totally new perspective on life. The ability to perceive objects in terms of energy patterns which interact with each other on a psychic level, and which can absorb thoughts, feelings and ideas, opens up a new dimension in the perception of 'the physical universe'.

Individuals differ in their ESP capabilities. Some may develop strong powers of clairvoyance or psychometry. Others excel at PK (psychokinesis) and healing. Still others may exhibit precognitive abilities. You could find that you are better at picking up psychic messages than you are at sending them. Or you may discover that you are an 'all-rounder', with equal talent in every department.

If you are worried that you are not spiritual or high-minded enough to be a healer, or that you lack the concentration to become a good psychometrist, let me assure you that neither spirituality nor great powers of concentration are required for any aspect of psychic development.

An individual's personality is not always reflected in the types of ESP they develop. For example, persons not noted for being emotionally sensitive sometimes turn out to be highly receptive psychically. And not all healers are magnanimous by nature. Rasputin, the so-called 'mad monk' was not, by all accounts, a very pleasant or spiritual character, yet he was undoubtedly a first-rate healer. It is my experience that the people with the most aptitude in this department are, more often than not, precisely those individuals who would never dream of developing this ability, or who would not even accept the reality of psychic healing.

Escapism and ESP

For many people, life is drab and uninteresting, with each day bringing the same predictable old routine. It is not unnatural, in such circumstances, to yearn for a more colourful and exciting way of life, and to look for it in the realms of the psychic and the paranormal. There is a universe of untapped power, an infinite resource within the psychic reach of every person – regardless of their physical restrictions – just waiting to be discovered and explored. Once it has been released, this power can transform the most mundane event into the most wonderful. The whole area of psychic study and development opens up entirely new possibilities in the quest for self-knowledge and consciousness exploration. But there is more to inner discovery than daydreaming and flights of fancy. Once you have become psychically attuned, your range of perception will be greatly increased and you will gain access to information and ideas that would otherwise remain beyond your reach. You must be careful, however, not to use your new-found psychic abilities merely as a means to escape from the everyday problems of your life. The psychic world *is not a separate reality*; it is an extension of the reality that we all share. Your involvement with the psychic realm should not interfere with or detract in any way from your mundane activities; rather, the insights you can gain through psychic attunement should contribute to the quality of your day-to-day life. Psychic development and self-improvement go hand in hand, and the exercises given in this book for ESP development will also work to polarize and strengthen some of the more positive aspects of your personality. They may not make you a 'better' person, but they should help you to become a stronger, more effective one. And, as your psychic abilities improve, so too will your powers of creative self-expression – in other words, your musical and artistic abilities will be considerably enhanced as your suprasensory powers come to the fore.

Psychic awareness spills over into all areas of life, and if you give the matter some thought you will realize that there is an infinite number of ways in which ESP can be utilized to enrich your life and enable you to achieve your ambitions, whether they be spiritual or materialistic. This being the case, it would be a great mistake to regard ESP merely as a form of escapism.

Increased psychic awareness is not a method of getting away from the world; *it is a means of becoming more involved with it.*

ESP and Spirituality

There are those to whom psychic matters are regarded in a spiritual or philosophical light. They see psychic awareness as an end in itself, a kind of inner meditation. This is all very well, but it must not be assumed that there is a direct connection between psychic power and spirituality: in my view, there is not. Many people are surprised to learn that the most talented psychics are seldom spiritual or unworldly individuals, but are more often strong individualists who are highly competitive, outgoing, materialistic and ambitious. This is not to say that a psychic cannot also be a spiritual or high-minded person – only that there is no direct link between ESP and spirituality.

CHAPTER TWO

ESP AND SCIENCE

From the Supernatural to the Paranormal

Until the latter half of the last century, any phenomenon that could not be explained according to the established laws of physics was labelled under the general heading of the supernatural. This term was used to describe a wide range of odd occurrences and strange events. Ghosts, fairies, magic spells, demoniac possession, second sight and prophecy were all classed as supernatural events.

When the supernatural – or, rather, certain aspects of the supernatural – became the subject of serious scientific study, the term was replaced with the more scientific-sounding title of 'the paranormal'. Although this term refers, in general, to the same phenomena previously referred to as supernatural, the word paranormal suggests a connection with the mind. And, whereas the term supernatural usually refers to phenomena that are essentially *beyond* explanation, the word 'paranormal' is widely understood to denote *that which has yet to be explained.*

Thus, phenomena that had previously been regarded in mystical or religious terms could now be considered in terms of physics and psychology, and accepted as scientifically respectable – or *almost* respectable – subjects for study.

There are more things in heaven and earth than we can understand, even in this technological age of enlightenment. Despite the fantastic achievements of science since the beginning of this century in the fields of chemistry, physics and medicine, scientists have failed miserably in their efforts to explain the nature of ESP and psychical phenomena.

When ESP first became the object of serious scientific study, in the late 1800s and early 1900s, it was generally assumed that the mysteries surrounding the subject would be resolved within the space of one, or at most two, decades. Such optimism is understandable when one remembers that this was at a time when it must have seemed as though scientists had found the key to unlock the secrets of the universe. In every other area of scientific endeavour, tremendous discoveries were being made almost daily. If moving pictures could be projected onto a screen; if the human voice could be transmitted hundreds of miles through the air; if man could fly ... then surely it was only a matter of time before scientists had tied up all the loose ends – including those of psychical phenomena.

Most scientists took the view that, if these phenomena were real, then it must be possible to explain them in logical, scientific terms and to analyse them by due scientific process. It was simply a question of approaching the subject in a rational, objective way; of systematically sifting through all the relevant pieces of information until nothing remained but the essential – and testable – facts. If, on the other hand – and this was considered far more likely – paranormal phenomena were illusory, then they would not stand up to critical, objective investigation, and scientists could dismiss them as superstition or mass hysteria.

Now, after more than a hundred years of scientific research into ESP, the phenomenon still has not been reduced to a mathematical formula, and the psychic riddle has not yet succumbed to the process of scientific analysis. In fact the very opposite has happened. Many of the more recent scientific discoveries have tended to support and confirm what psychics and mystics have been saying all along: the clinical studies of 'out-of-the-body' experiences reported by near-death hospital patients have given new credence to the concepts of astral projection and life-after-death; the invention of the Kirlian, or high-voltage 'camera', has made it possible to take colour photographs of something that distinctly resembles the human aura which clairvoyants have always claimed to be able to see; and the discovery that plants can 'feel' and respond to human emotions has taken the notion of a gardener's 'green thumb' out of the realms of superstition and into the textbooks of science.

Acupuncture, the ancient Chinese healing system based on the manipulation of invisible psychic energy centres on the surface of the body, is now a widely accepted form of medical treatment. And the meridian lines – the channels along which this vital energy flows – the reality of which was denied by most doctors and scientists only a few decades ago, can now be detected and measured with sensitive electronic equipment.

Astrology, too, has become a more creditable pursuit since the advent of statistical analysis by computer, and it has now been established beyond any reasonable doubt that the planets do, after all, exert some influence over human events, or at least that there is some synchronicity between their movements and events on earth.

Many of the superstitions of a mere fifty years ago have now become accepted, scientific facts. Science has turned full circle: instead of solving the age-old mysteries of time and space and the human psyche, it has instead confirmed the reality of many strange phenomena – and provided us with still more imponderables. Space, it would now seem, is curved. Time is relative. Particles of matter can vanish and reappear at different points in space. The universe, we are informed, is expanding. Anti-matter is a reality. Even the terminology of space-age science reflects the change of mood that is now taking place: 'strangeness' and 'charm' are terms now used to describe unknown quantities in physics.

Gradually and reluctantly scientists are moving towards a world-view that is closer to that of the mystic than that of the materialist. The same thing is happening in the field of medicine, where orthodox techniques are in many cases being rejected in favour of natural and intuitive methods.

Hopefully, it will be possible – for the first time ever – to achieve a balance between these two approaches in the not-too-distant future.

Many theories have been put forward to account for ESP, and a great deal of serious research has been carried out into the subject since the beginning of the century. Unfortunately, this research has been almost exclusively directed towards finding physical proof for the existence of psychical phenomena, rather than trying to understand the nature and the mechanics of ESP.

Since this book is intended primarily as a practical guide to psychic development, I do not propose to dwell on the theoretical aspects of the subject. There are many excellent books available which deal with psychical phenomena from that angle. However, it is necessary to touch on the theory and the background of ESP research for the benefit of those readers who are new to the subject.

In the early 1930s Dr J. B. Rhine succeeded in making ESP research – or parapsychology as it was soon to become known – a scientifically respectable pursuit, when he founded the Institute of Parapsychological Research at Duke University in North Carolina, USA. It was the first institution of its kind to receive official recognition.

Dr Rhine, formerly a botanist, had a novel if somewhat laborious approach to the investigation of ESP. Realizing that it was practically impossible to scientifically evaluate spontaneous psychical phenomena – since the circumstances and conditions differed in every case – Rhine set about conducting experiments under controlled conditions, reducing the variable factors to an absolute minimum. In this way, results of experiments could be quantified, and the evidence for or against ESP could be evaluated on a statistical basis. The prime requisite for any phenomenon to be scientifically acceptable is repeatability, and Rhine hoped to prove the existence of ESP as a statistical constant. Whether or not he succeeded in this is still a matter for debate. He carried out thousands of experiments under these carefully controlled conditions (although, it must be said that there are those who have expressed doubts about the care with which these controls were set up), using as his subjects not well-known psychics but men and women – and of course children – from all walks of life. It was Rhine who popularized the term 'extrasensory perception', or ESP, and it was he who first used the famous Zener cards, comprising the five symbols: cross, circle, star, wavy lines and square – which have since become the trademark of all things connected with this subject.

Rhine's test results were recorded in terms of percentages above and below chance expectancy. Thus, in a simple test into 'thought-transference' using the five Zener symbols as targets, a subject could be expected to guess one card in every five correctly, which would represent a score of 20 per cent. If the same test was carried out thousands of times and a subject was able to score consistently higher than this average, it would be possible to infer the existence of some kind of ESP, and to express this as a constant percentage above chance expectancy. After conducting many thousands of tests into telepathy, clairvoyance and precognition, Rhine eventually announced that he had found overwhelming statistical evidence for ESP. However, other paranormal researchers who attempted to duplicate his experiments obtained mixed results, and Rhine's experimental methods were heavily criticized by his fellow scientists, who claimed, among other things, that he had failed to take adequate

precautions against trickery and deception on the part of his subjects.

In more recent years there has been a more flexible and imaginative approach to ESP research, and the emphasis has shifted from merely trying to find evidence for the reality of the phenomenon to discovering the conditions in which it most often occurs, and identifying personality and character traits common to high scorers in psychic tests.

CHAPTER THREE

ESP —
THE SIXTH SENSE?

ESP has come to be regarded as a human faculty, or latent mental ability. The very term 'extrasensory perception' implies the existence of a sixth or extra sense. There is, however, no evidence at all to suggest that this is really the case. In fact, it is rather curious that this notion has persisted for so long, when all the signs point in an entirely different direction.

The most obvious refutation of the idea of ESP as a human faculty is the fact that many of the best-authenticated instances of psychical phenomena involve animals, insects and even plants. There are numerous well-documented accounts of household pets – particularly cats – that, having been left behind when their owners moved house, were able to find their way to the new home, sometimes over distances of many hundreds of miles.

Animals can very often sense impending danger, long before there are any physical indications that anything is amiss. A good example of this – and there are many – is the precognitive powers that birds display when they avoid perching on the branches of a tree which is about to be struck by lightning.

Just recently I noted a novel example of what appeared to be ESP among birds. Every day for several weeks I took the same London underground train, and every day the train 'rested' in a particular station, for five or ten minutes (the duration varied from day to day). As soon as the sliding doors opened, when the train came to a halt, in came the pigeons, scavenging on the crumbs of potato crisps dropped on the floor by passengers. Then, just seconds before the doors slid shut – and before the engine came to life – they hopped back out onto the platform.

I observed this ritual at least a dozen times, and never once did I see a pigeon trapped on the train when the doors closed. There are countless examples of this kind of thing on record. In the insect world, the ability of ants to communicate with each other and behave 'with a single mind' is difficult to explain in anything other than psychic terms.

Paranormal researchers have always tended to overlook the animal connection in their efforts to explain ESP, and, despite the overwhelming evidence of psychic ability among animals, birds and insects, many paranormalists insist that ESP is a new stage in our evolutionary development; the emergence of a new, sixth sense. This idea has appeal, but it is, unfortunately, without foundation. From what we know about ESP it would seem far more likely that it is a talent that we have either failed to develop or forgotten how to use at some stage in our distant past.

When we look down the evolutionary ladder, we can find increased evidence of psychic power. Even among members of our own species, it is those races of people that we regard as most primitive – i.e., less technologically advanced and less 'educated' – that are possessed of strong powers of ESP. The Australian aborigines, for instance, are renowned for their psychic feats. It is also notable that children, particularly those under the age of six, score consistently better than most adults in experiments into ESP.

It seems clear that ESP is not a sixth sense, but a *prime* sense; a faculty which can, under certain conditions, override the normal sensory process. Far from being a product of human intelligence or cerebral activity, it is apparent that this faculty actually *diminishes* with the process of intellectualization.

The sensory process which enables us to focus our intelligence also narrows our range of perception, and *inhibits* rather than enhances psychic awareness. The more complex or sophisticated the organism becomes, the less aptitude it has for psychic functioning.

CHAPTER FOUR

TYPES OF ESP

ESP is not my favourite term. I much prefer the Greek 'psi' (mind-soul), which can be more loosely applied. However, the term ESP is the one that most people are familiar with, and, after some deliberation (and the toss of a coin) it is the one that I have decided to use throughout this book. As I hope to show here, the terminology of the psychic sciences ought not to be taken too seriously in any case.

I have reached a personal compromise by using the term ESP to denote 'extra special perception' – which is a perfectly good description of the psychic faculty.

The term ESP is usually applied to three distinct types of psychical phenomena:

Telepathy   –   Direct mind-to-mind communication.

Clairvoyance   –   The power or ability to 'see' objects and events at a distance, without having recourse to the normal sensory channels of communication.

Precognition   –   The faculty of acquiring knowledge of future events by paranormal means.

The term ESP is sometimes used to include *retrocognition* (clairvoyant knowledge of past events) and *psychokinesis* or PK (the ability to move or affect objects by mind power: I would include psychic healing in this category).

Whilst these distinctions are useful for the purpose of study and discussion, it is important to note that telepathy, clairvoyance, precognition and so on, are not, as far as we know, separate phenomena, but different aspects of the same phenomenon – ESP. In reality – and in the laboratory – it is extremely difficult, if not impossible, to differentiate between one ESP effect and another. This is a very important point to note, and one which is often overlooked by even the most experienced psychical researchers.

Consider the following. You have a vivid dream in which you are reunited with your long-lost cousin, who emigrated to Australia many years ago and has not been seen or heard of since. You think nothing of your dream until the following day, when your doorbell rings and your long-lost cousin is standing on your doorstep.

The chronicles of paranormal research are crammed with events of this kind. Such apparently psychic occurrences can never be acceptable as scientific proof of ESP, no matter how well-verified or dramatic they may be, since the possibility of fraud or coincidence cannot be entirely ruled out. Such examples of spontaneous ESP form the backdrop of convincing circumstantial evidence for the reality of the phenomenon.

If, however, we accept that your dream is a genuine paranormal event, into which category of ESP does it fit? This is where we run into trouble with our neat little definitions. As you may have realized, your ESP dream can be classified under any one of the three main headings given above:

Precognition	–	In your dream you foresaw an event that would subsequently take place.
Telepathy	–	Your cousin, who would, of course, have been thinking about you, communicated his intention of visiting you, via telepathy.
Clairvoyance	–	You psychically divined the near presence of your cousin as you slept.

From this it can be seen that the labels we ascribe to the various ESP effects are not as clear-cut or well-defined as they may at first appear to be.

In controlled experiments in the laboratory, researchers take elaborate and painstaking precautions to try to determine precisely which type of ESP is being produced. In tests to establish clairvoyance, for example, great care is taken to ensure that none of the participants in the test – including the experimenters themselves – can have any way of knowing the contents of the target material (the information that is to be psychically discovered).

Mechanical devices are used to shuffle cards, toss dice and select random numbers, pictures or words to be used as targets. By using electronic random-selection devices, it is possible to eliminate the possibility of telepathy – but not precognition.

In telepathic experiments there is another complication: in order to preclude the possibility of error or deception, target material must be recorded in some way, for later verification. This means that there is no foolproof way to ensure that the recipient in such an experiment (i.e. the subject on the receiving end of the hoped-for telepathic exchange) is actually gleaning the information by telepathy, and is not perceiving the written, taped or computer-coded target material by precognition or direct clairvoyance. Furthermore, in all kinds of ESP experiments, it is virtually impossible to rule out the presence of PK.

From this it can be seen that it is practically impossible to establish the existence of specific types of ESP in isolation using current methods of experimentation.

If you are to gain any understanding of this subject, you must become aware of the limitations of the terminology available and the tenuity of the descriptions and definitions used in connection with ESP and psychic matters in general.

Telepathy, clairvoyance and precognition are terms used to describe these different aspects of a single phenomenon. There is no evidence to suggest that they exist independently. Yet many researchers have succumbed to the temptation to study these ESP effects in isolation, as distinct and separate phenomena.

The effect that most people find easiest to accept – particularly the more scientific-minded – is telepathy. Presumably this is because it is possible to make a plausible comparison between 'telepathic transmission' and radio transmission. It is worth noting that the first experiments into radio transmission took place at a time when there was tremendous interest in psychic matters, and especially in mind-to-mind communication: the invention of the radio probably did more than anything else to promote a belief in 'mental telepathy'. After all, if information could be transmitted from one electronic device to another over long distances, then surely it was also possible for the human brain – itself an electrical device – to send and receive messages by a similar process?

In fact there is no evidence whatever to substantiate the idea that psychic or mental impressions are transmitted in the same way that radio waves are. No telepathic 'waves' have ever been detected. Nor is there any more proof for telepathy in general than there is for other ESP effects like clairvoyance, PK and precognition.

Since telepathy, clairvoyance and precognition are all aspects of the same, overall phenomenon of ESP, and since they cannot be distinguished either in the laboratory or when they occur spontaneously, it follows that if there is a theory to explain one of these aspects, it must also account for the others. In other words, if a theory is put forward to explain telepathy, it must also go a long way towards explaining precognition, since the two are not distinct phenomena but different ESP qualities. This may seem to be quite obvious, and I do not wish to belabour the point, but it is a fact that, time and again, paranormalists carrying out research into ESP have become preoccupied with a particular aspect of the phenomenon; very often it is telepathy – the most rational face of ESP – for which they advance loose theories which are usually variations on the 'mental radio' theme.

Until recently the most widely held theory held by psychical researchers in relation to ESP centered around this idea that the human mind can, under certain conditions, operate in much the same way as a radio transmitter–receiver, and that the agency by which thoughts are sent and received is essentially electrical in nature. On the face of it, this theory seems quite reasonable. The human brain is, after all, similar to a computer in many respects, with a working capacity of 15 billion cells – and it works by an electrical process. It is not unreasonable to suppose that some of the brain's electrical impulses may be converted into radio waves which could be picked up by others tuned in to the same wavelength.

This theory has great appeal for the orthodox man of science. The evidence available, however, does not support it. On the contrary, everything that is known about radio waves, electricity and telepathy goes against this possibility. To begin with, numerous experiments have indicated that 'telepathic transmission' does not seem to be affected by distance; experiments in which sender and receiver were thousands of miles apart have yielded excellent results. Secondly, it is highly unlikely that the tiny amount of electricity that the human brain is capable of producing – scarcely enough to illuminate a small pocket torch – could be transmitted hundreds or thousands of miles without dissipating (with electricity, distance makes the charge grow weaker). Even the world's most powerful radio transmitters are limited by the curvature of the earth, and require the aid of space satellites to carry the signal over long distances.

Thirdly, excellent results have been obtained in ESP experiments in which the participants were surrounded by electrical shielding devices designed to block all known types of electromagnetic waves. In some tests into general ESP, the use of these electric screens actually seemed to enhance, rather than inhibit psychic perception – a fact that would indicate a *connection* between ESP and electromagnetism, though not an explanation of the phenomenon.

Finally, and this is the most crucial point of all, even if we were to assume that the human brain is somehow capable of transmitting and receiving messages in the way described, and even if these transmissions are of such a nature that they can travel long distances and penetrate electrical shielding devices, the theory would not account for those other types of ESP with which telepathy is inextricably linked.

CHAPTER FIVE

THE NATURE OF ESP

Perhaps on account of its early associations with mesmerism and the nineteenth-century stage 'mentalist', ESP has come to be regarded as a hidden faculty of the mind; a dormant sixth sense which, for reasons unknown, becomes highly developed in a few rare individuals.

Research has shown that ESP ability can be linked with certain personality types and with specific character and even physical traits. And there is evidence to suggest that, in order to effect psychic transmission – or telepathy – the brain of the recipient must be functioning on an electrical frequency that is characterized by the production of Alpha waves. (The human brain operates on four basic levels or in four different 'gears' – Alpha, Beta, Delta and Theta. Alpha rhythm occurs naturally when you are in a meditative or relaxed state.)

Although it is possible to link ESP with specific mental processes, it does not follow that the brain is the source of psychic perception, as some researchers have concluded. My own observations have led me to the view that ESP is a universal characteristic, common to *all things*, and is not merely a mental faculty. There is no contradiction here. There are a number of processes that we normally associate with the brain but which are, in fact, universal processes. Memory is a good example. We tend to regard memory as a function of the brain – a mental, even human, process – but this is not really the case. All things – people, animals, insects, plants and even 'inanimate' objects – have the capacity to remember. An ant can remember its way back to its nest just as efficiently as a man can remember his route home. The process is the same in both cases; only the level of awareness is different. The ability of a rubber band to return to its original shape when stretched and released is also an act of memory. And the ability of any object to maintain its form when it is constantly surrounded by destructive forces is another example of the memory process. The fact that we humans are capable of a more sophisticated ability of review does not alter the fact that the process is not essentially a cerebral one.

Similarly, the fact that we equate ESP with mental or psychological factors does not mean that the brain is the source of the phenomenon: in my view it is not. ESP is a *universal* characteristic, a quality common to all things. It is not a mental faculty. When I talk about ESP development, I refer to the ability – the mental ability – to become *aware* of psychic impressions, and to learn to *distinguish* these impressions from non-psychic ones. ESP is not a gift bestowed upon a few special individuals; it is a power shared by all living things.

Furthermore, the ESP process is a constant one: even as you read these words, you are psychically sending and receiving information about people and things outside the range of your sensory perception. Fortunately, you are not conscious of this low level ESP activity. Why 'fortunately'? Just imagine what would happen if you were to gain instant and total access to this function: your conscious mind would be flooded with a vast amount of information from a million different sources – and most of it would be meaningless to you. You would pick up the thoughts and emotions of tens of thousands of people all at once. Furthermore, you would be unable to distinguish these thoughts from your own, since they would have arrived in your mind by way of your subconscious and would therefore have bypassed the critical mind which normally filters, evaluates, modifies and 'pegs' information received via the basic senses. Your mind simply could not cope with such an overload – which is one very good reason for you to avoid psychic development programmes that promise to 'open the floodgates' of your dormant powers: they just might succeed.

Psychic communication takes place constantly at deep mind level. The instant you think about someone, you establish a psychic link with them. Unless the person concerned is particularly sensitive to such impressions, they will not be conscious of this communication. However, the contact will register at deep mind level, and there may also be measurable physical reactions such as raised blood volume and increased muscular tension. It is interesting to note that one of the first parts of the body to register raised blood volume is the ear lobe – which gives new significance to the 'superstition' that a burning sensation in the ears indicates that the individual concerned is the subject of some distant discussion.

If the psychic message is to be received and translated on a conscious level, it must be clearly defined and as uncomplicated as possible – and it must be accompanied by a powerful psychic 'voltage'. These aspects will be dealt with later.

Exercise 1

This exercise should be carried out in a dimly lit room (not completely dark) at a time when there is no possibility of your being disturbed. The room should be warm and well-ventilated (most psychic exercises and experiments involve you remaining motionless in a darkened room for fairly long periods, therefore it is important to ensure that the room is comfortably warm, but not roasting. Remember, physical immobility causes the body's temperature to drop).

Sit upright in a *hard-backed* chair, with your feet together on the floor and your hands folded *loosely* in front of you. Close your eyes and simply sit there for a few minutes, allowing your thoughts to wander as they will.

Open your eyes again and become aware of the details of your surroundings. Carefully study everything in your range of vision – but do not shift your position. Study the floor, the walls, the various objects in the room. Make a mental note of as many details as you can. Next, expand your attention to become aware of your general location. 'See' the rest of the building in your mind's eye; the street outside, the whole area ... Send your mind on an aerial reconnaissance of the city or countryside around you. Get a strong sense of your exact location.

Mentally return to the room, and once again probe it with your senses. Don't just see it: smell, taste, hear and feel everything around you. Try to extend your senses. 'Feel' the walls from your chair. 'Taste' the air in your room. Strain your ears for the slightest creak of furniture, the tiniest whisper from the bookcase. Become conscious of the force of gravity holding you in your chair. Feel the pressure of the air on your skin. Listen for the beat of your heart. *Do not* make any attempt to analyse these sensations; simply note them for what they are.

After ten or fifteen minutes, close your eyes again and go through the mental reconnaissance process once more, this time keeping your eyes closed. 'See' the room, the furniture and so on, in your mind. Visualize your surroundings as clearly and in as much detail as you can. (Most people find it very difficult to visualize anything clearly, so do not worry if you have trouble holding the image in your mind at first. Visualization ability improves with practice.)

After five or ten minutes of this, take a few deep breaths and end the exercise.

Most people have lost touch with their senses. The object of this exercise is to enable you to become more familiar with the range of your sensory process, and to strengthen your sense of self-location. You must reach the boundaries of your physical senses before you can break through them.

This exercise should be carried out two or three times a week, for twenty minutes to one hour at a time.

CHAPTER SIX

RELAXATION AND ESP

If there is a 'key' to psychic development, it is relaxation. There are a number of reasons why this is so:

1. A relaxed body cannot contain a destructive emotion. This means that it is impossible to relax and worry at the same time (for this reason alone the ability to become perfectly relaxed at will is a most valuable asset). As we shall see, control over the emotions is of paramount importance when it comes to sending and receiving information psychically.

2. When the body is at rest, the field of consciousness expands, and the vital energies are available to the mind. Energy that would otherwise be used by the body can be 'stepped up' and redirected to the higher faculties. The power of thought – that is, the power available for mental and psychic functioning – is greatly increased when the state of total relaxation is achieved.

3. With controlled, deep relaxation, thoughts become crystal clear, and it is possible to hold mental images for long periods. Clarity of thought is essential to the control of the psychic process, and in the area of telepathy the advantage of being able to hold onto thought-images will be obvious. If you are to 'see' the thoughts of others, it will help if you are first able to see your own thoughts clearly. The word clairvoyance actually means 'clear vision', and it is just as important – perhaps even more important – to be able to see inwards as it is to see outwards.

4. You have often heard it said that a blind man develops a 'sixth

sense' to compensate for his lack of sight. There is some truth in this. When one sense is 'switched off', the others tend to become sharper, more acute. This is the reason why people close their eyes when listening for some delicate sound, or when trying to remember something. The available energy is redistributed when the senses are switched off, and the higher faculties come into play. Paradoxically, the unused or resting senses also become more acute.

5. Total relaxation brings increased mind control, and it is an important part of psychic training to be able to produce specific mental states (or specific brain rhythms) at will.

6. When the mind is free from the necessity to monitor and regulate the workings of the body (vital functions will not be affected by even the deepest relaxation), and when it is rid of the 'noise' or interference from the surface mind, it can pick up and identify impressions of the most fleeting or subtle nature. Just as it is possible to hear the slightest whisper when there is complete silence, so it is possible to detect minute psychic signals when the mind is calm and unruffled.

Perhaps you, like many people, regard the prospect of doing relaxation exercises tedious and unexciting. If so, I urge you to reconsider your ideas on the subject. Relaxation is not just a matter of 'not doing anything', it is a positive state which only a very few people ever experience, let alone learn how to produce at will.

Many people are convinced that they are able to relax completely. Almost invariably, they are mistaken. Mastering the art of perfect relaxation is the most important step you must take towards developing your psychic powers.

The following, simple technique, has been tried and tested over a good many years. Study it well, and practise it regularly. The best time to carry out relaxation exercises is when you are alert and refreshed, and *not* when you are feeling tired. If you do this exercise at night, in bed, you will probably fall asleep before you are halfway through it – which is good news if you happen to be an insomniac.

Tension

Essentially, there are two kinds of tension – a fact that is seldom acknowledged in books dealing with the subject. Hold your index finger straight out in front of you. Now bend it, and keep it bent. The muscles of that finger are now tensed, which is to say electrical energy is being discharged into them, causing them to contract. This may be said to be 'benign' tension, since the nervous energy used is released in a controlled action.

Now straighten the finger again, and *think* about bending it, but don't – that is, *threaten* to bend it. This readiness produces an electrical potential in the muscles of the finger, but, until you actually bend the finger, the potential will not be properly discharged. This can be compared to applying a car's brakes and accelerator simultaneously; you burn up a lot of fuel unnecessarily, you cause wear and tear to the 'engine', and you get nowhere fast. The constant presence of undischarged electrical energy in a group of muscles causes all kinds of chemical and organic imbalances that ultimately result in permanent damage to the system. This is destructive tension; it poisons the body and interferes with the flow of vital energy.

Destructive tension becomes a habit that is difficult to break. Check yourself right now – are you tensing your shoulders? Your jaw? Your forehead? A muscle should not be tensed unless it is working. Whenever you become aware of tension in a muscle or group of muscles, you should immediately *tense that muscle even more* than it is already. Accentuate the tension; 'go into it', and by doing so you can isolate it and bring it under your conscious control. Then you can relax it.

Tension impedes the flow of psychic energy like a knot in a hosepipe impedes the flow of water. You must begin to unblock all channels by learning to become aware of the presence of tension in your body. Check yourself as often as you remember to do so, and relax consciously.

Before you can learn how to relax fully, you must first learn to become aware of tension. Until you can recognize tension in a group of muscles, you cannot be sure when those muscles are in a relaxed state. For this reason, the position you adopt for the following relaxation exercise *should not be comfortable*. It is far easier to identify a relaxed muscle when physical pressure is applied. This is one of the reasons why the Indian fakir lies on a bed of nails to relax and meditate, rather than a soft mattress. It is better, therefore, if you sit in a hard-backed chair, or lie on the floor to do the exercise, rather than in a comfortable armchair or couch.

If you have a friend to help you with this exercise, it is a good idea to get him or her to pinch various parts of your body – not too hard – when you feel you are fully relaxed. If there is still some tension in the area pinched, you will become conscious of it (it will probably hurt), and be able to correct it. If the area is properly relaxed you should be aware of a slight analgesic effect – i.e. the pinch will be less painful than it would normally be. This is because a relaxed body has a much greater resistance to pain and injury (which is also why a drunkard who falls over a dozen times on his way home is far less likely to hurt himself or break any bones than a person who stumbles while sober).

Technique for Perfect Relaxation

Carry out this exercise at a time and in a place where you will not be disturbed. The room should be warm and well-ventilated. Remember, your body surface temperature will drop considerably during the exercise.

1. Lie on a hard surface (or, if you prefer, sit in a hard-backed chair).

    Lie quite still for several minutes, keeping your eyes open. The room should be dimly lit, but not in darkness. Keep your hands by your sides and your legs uncrossed. (Incidentally, you should always avoid clasping your hands or crossing your legs during psychic readings, as this interferes with the flow of psychic energy.)

    Now, imagine that you are beginning to 'set', like a cement or jelly. Imagine that you are capable of less and less movement until, finally, your body is completely motionless. Do not move a muscle. This may not be as easy as it sounds; the brain is lazy, particularly when it comes to any kind of sustained effort, and it will do its best to get you to shift your position – to scratch your nose (it will produce an itch), yawn, swallow, etc. You must resist the urge to do any of these things. Instead, you must remain absolutely still for a full five minutes. If you feel uncomfortable, this is all the better.

2. Close your eyes and do a mental tour of your body, starting at your toes and working up to the top of your head. Give special attention to the muscles of your shoulders, neck and jaws. Do not, at this stage, make any attempt to relax the various parts of your body; simply become aware of each group of muscles and make a mental note of how tensed or relaxed they feel. This tour of inspection should take about three minutes to complete.

3. Now, take a few deep breaths, *in through your mouth and out through your nose*, emptying your lungs completely each time. Then breathe normally again, through your nose.

4. Tense the toes of your left foot as tightly as possible, and hold the tension for ten seconds. Relax these muscles and *immediately* tense the toes of your *right* foot. Hold the tension for ten seconds then relax the muscles and *immediately* switch your attention to your left calf, tensing the muscles here for ten seconds ... let go and *immediately* tense the right calf muscles ... and so on with every part of the body, each time tensing the muscles for ten seconds then letting go and switching to a different group of muscles. You should complete this sequence by knitting your brow – hold, and relax. It is important that the switch of attention – and tension – is *immediate*.

5. At this stage you should attend to your breathing. Begin by simply listening to the sound of the air moving through your nostrils: *feel* the air filling and vacating your lungs. *Gradually* take longer and deeper breaths, and try to breathe without making any sound, smoothly, evenly and silently.

Breathe into your 'tummy', or lower chest, at the beginning of each inhalation, filling your upper chest last. When you exhale, empty your upper chest first, then the lower chest. Try to do all this in one smooth movement. Be sure to exhale fully each time. It should take a couple of seconds longer to exhale than to inhale. If you breathe in to a count of eight, you should exhale to a count of ten.

6. Become aware of the force of gravity pulling your body downwards. Feel your own weight; feel the weight of your fingers, hands, arms, legs and head.

7. You have probably seen those Dracula movies where the Count is exposed to a lethal dose of daylight, whereupon his body begins to disintegrate before your very eyes, and within minutes there is nothing left of him but a pile of dust. You must now imagine that the same process of disintegration is happening to you. Visualize your body beginning to crumble. Feel your fingers, then your hands, then your arms turning to dust. Imagine, as vividly as you can, that your whole body is turning into a fine powder on the floor (or chair). If you have followed the preceding instructions properly you should have little trouble in imagining this; sometimes the 'turning to dust' sensation occurs spontaneously with the onset of deep relaxation.

8. You have become a pile of dust. Now, imagine that there is a light breeze and that it is gently blowing what is left of you away, scattering you in all directions ... until there is nothing remaining – but your consciousness.

9. When you are ready, give yourself the instruction, either mentally or aloud: 'Whenever I count from ten down to one and say the word *Omega* (or any other key word you want to use) three times, *I will immediately become perfectly relaxed*, as I am at this moment.' Repeat this instruction several times.

10. To end the exercise, take a deep breath and stretch your body gently. Say aloud to yourself: 'At the count of three, I will open my eyes and be fully awake, alert and refreshed.' You can give yourself positive self-suggestions at this point – for example: 'From now on my memory will improve' or, '... my concentration will get better' – or even, '... my psychic abilities will improve.'

'One ... two ... three ...'

Open your eyes. Shrug your shoulders. Stretch your legs. Clench and unclench your hands a few times, then *slowly* stand up.

After doing this exercise for the first time you will probably feel a bit stiff – so do not make any sudden movements for a while, or you could pull a muscle – but you should also feel extremely relaxed and refreshed (unless it is close to your bedtime anyway, in which case you should sleep like a top).

Before you carry out this relaxation technique, you must first *memorize* the instructions given: you will not be able to refer to them when you are halfway through the routine.

1.   Remain motionless.
2.   Mental tour, noting tension.
3.   Deep breaths.
4.   Tense and relax sequence.
5.   Listen and control your breathing.
6.   Feel your weight.
7.   'Turning to dust'.
8.   Blown away...
9.   Mental instructions and signal.
10.   End on count of three.

If you carry out this exercise regularly, you will instil a conditioned reflex response to your signal, so that ultimately it will not be necessary to go through the whole routine: simply by counting from ten down to one and uttering the 'magic word', you will immediately become totally relaxed and, consequently, highly receptive to psychic impressions.

CHAPTER SEVEN

INTUITION

Intuition v. Logic

In common with other forms of creative ability, psychic awareness is a natural part of our development. As children we take part in exercises to increase our ESP powers. These take the form of games such as 'Blind Man's Buff', 'I Spy' and 'Pin the Tail on the Donkey'. Games like these promote *instinctive*, intuitive responses, rather than rational or logical assessments. This stage in our development is also marked by strong powers of creative imagery.

Both these aspects of our psychic growth are systematically supressed. We are chastised for 'imagining things' and for 'exaggerating'.

We are soon programmed to make 'value judgements' based on the facts available. We are taught that there is only one valid way to make an assessment: by the process of logical deduction. And when there is insufficient information available to make such an assessment, we are taught to reserve judgement. All intuitive and instinctive behaviour is actively – if not forcibly – discouraged. This negative programming is so effective that most adults find it extremely difficult to 'guess blind' about anything, or to accept any evaluation that has no basis in logic.

At school we were constantly advised to be methodical, and the problems we were given to work out were problems of logic and deduction, not *real* problems – i.e. the factors we were presented with were compatible with the processes we were expected to use to reach the solution. The possibility that there might be alternative ways of dealing with the problem, or that there could be more than one possible answer, is never admitted. The framework is inflexible. At school, I was chastised for giving solutions to mathematical problems without showing the deductive process by which I was supposed to reach the solution. There was no allowance for the possibility of other, non-deductive processes which could arrive at the same conclusion. The fact that the answer was correct counted for nothing.

Although the situation has improved somewhat in recent years, with a greater emphasis on learning through discovery, the process of education for children still has more to do with brainwashing than with increasing their powers of intelligence and creativity. Children are not encouraged to think; they are trained to think *in a certain way*. There is very little scope, in the present system, for the development of the intuitive faculties. Hence it is not surprising that children, as we have seen, possess stronger ESP powers than adults, and that their psychic abilities tend to fall off sharply when the process of education begins.

The Mme Za Za Effect

Some years ago I went to see a show given by a conjuror who specialized in so-called 'mental magic' – which is to say he used trickery to give the illusion of clairvoyance and mindreading. He admitted, at the beginning of his act, that all his effects were achieved by misdirection, sleight of hand and simple psychology, and he made no claim to real psychic abilities.

I had an opportunity to speak to him after the show, and he told me that he had always been interested in genuine psychical phenomena, but had only ever had one noteworthy experience of this kind. It occurred on the stage, when he was doing his 'mindreading' act. The idea of the trick was that a member of the audience would write a three-digit number on a slip of paper which he, the conjuror, would try to pick up by 'telepathy'. On this particular occasion, however, the trick went wrong, when a slip of paper that was to be switched went missing. The unfortunate fellow didn't know what to do next. The audience waited with bated breath as he pretended to concentrate intensely. The minutes ticked by, until finally, in sheer desperation, he called out the first three-digit number that came into his head. The audience was amazed, but not nearly as much as he himself was, when the number turned out to be correct.

'The strange thing is,' he told me, 'as I called out the number – in that instant – I *knew* with absolute certainty that it was the right number.'

This was a perfect example of 'crisis ESP', more of which later. I was interested enough in this story to check up to see if other conjurors had had similar experiences. I was not too surprised to discover that it is a fairly common occurrence for stage mentalists to suddenly acquire genuine ESP powers which come to the fore when their mindreading tricks go wrong. It had even happened to the arch sceptic of psychic matters, Harry Houdini, during a performance he was giving to demonstrate how bogus mediums used trickery to dupe their sitters.

I decided to carry out some private experiments into this phenomenon, and, at a meeting of a psychic study group with which I was involved, I organized a role-playing game in which every person present took a turn at playing the part of 'Madame Za Za, who knows all and sees all'. As I suspected, most of them were able to give first-rate demonstrations of clairvoyance and psychometry in this role – much to their own surprise.

I repeated this experiment on numerous occasions, usually with the same good results. I also discovered that many professional psychics first became aware of their powers while playing the part of the fortune-teller at charity bazaars and fêtes. One leading lady clairvoyant told me how she discovered her previously unsuspected psychic abilities while playing the "Madame Za Za' role at a school fête:

'I was all dressed up, gypsy style, with a sequinned headscarf and huge circular earrings. My first customer was a young woman who was, I later found out, a teacher at the school. I took both of her hands and pretended to scrutinize them closely, as I imagined a real palmist would. In fact, I knew nothing at all about palmistry, and I was desperately trying to think of something to say – but my mind was a complete blank, despite the fact that I had rehearsed my "spiel" all week.

'Finally, after several long minutes of mutual embarrassment during which I must have said 'hmm, that's interesting' at least a dozen times, I suddenly heard myself saying: 'You are married to a man who is a foreigner, and you are having a secret affair with an older man whose initial is M.'

Even as I spoke, I wanted to bite my tongue. To my great surprise, however, the young woman turned pale and admitted at once that what I had said was correct. I was stunned by what I thought must have been a lucky guess.

'But the same thing happened with the next person I saw, and the one after that. Most of what I said was just waffle, but every now and again I picked up these "flashes" which were far more accurate than chance would have allowed.'

There are two points to be noted from these examples. First of all, it is clear that ESP works best *when it has to work* – i.e. when there is no other source of information for the brain to act upon. The stage mentalist had no choice but to come up with a number, otherwise he would have looked very foolish. And the lady clairvoyant referred to above had to say something to relieve an increasingly embarrassing situation.

These are situations of intense personal crisis, and it is this *crisis factor* which is so often present in the most impressive instances of precognition, telepathy and clairvoyance.

Secondly, ESP comes to the fore when it has an appropriate outlet or means of expression, and when there is some kind of framework in which it is *permitted* to work. An individual who might otherwise feel inhibited about making 'wild' predictions, may do so readily in the guise of Mme Za Za.

CHAPTER EIGHT

TRAINING THE MIND

Concentration and ESP

Psychics in fiction and stage mindreaders are constantly exhorting people to concentrate on numbers, names and messages to be picked up telepathically. 'Concentrate harder!' is the familiar command of the platform mentalist to his assistant when he appears to be having difficulty receiving the communication. In reality, mental concentration is the very opposite of the state of mind required for most types of psi-functioning.

To concentrate, in the usual meaning of the term, is to focus one's attention sharply on a specific subject or idea; to apply the critical faculties. This is precisely what you have to avoid when you want to elicit ESP. Instead, you should be aiming for a feeling of slight detachment and mental diffusion; soft focus rather than sharp definition. Concentration requires *effort*, and effort involves *tension* – and, as we have seen, tension negates psychic receptivity.

Try this simple test: think of a number, then close your eyes and concentrate on it as hard as you can for half a minute. Do it now. Concentration is essentially a muscular action, rather than a mental exercise. To 'concentrate harder' is to increase the level of muscular tension that accompanies the mental state. Did you squeeze your eyes tightly shut as you concentrated on your number? Did you wrinkle your brow, grit your teeth or clench your fists? Most people do all of these things when they want to hold a certain thought in their mind: in fact, the tension involved is counterproductive to clear thinking – and to clairvoyance.

Guess Power

As I have said, childhood and later conditioning has made it extremely difficult for most people to make 'wild' guesses or predictions. The brain has a well-established circuitry for dealing with the problems and decisions that it has to deal with. Invariably, the mental process follows the route of least resistance; the evidence is weighed up in an instant and an immediate, logical evaluation is made.

Unless this familiar pattern is disrupted – unless the critical mind is bypassed – there is little chance of establishing a new, 'ESP route'. *The psychic faculties come to the fore when other modes of perception and assessment are unavailable* – so, you must learn – or relearn – how to make decisions that are not based on logical deduction from the available facts. You must start *guessing* about things and responding to situations *instinctively*. By doing this you create an opening to be filled by your latent psychic abilities; you produce a mental framework in which it is possible to respond to events in an intuitive way.

Your guesses must be wild, not calculated.

For starters, see if you can guess the identity of the next person to call you on the telephone. Straightaway you will probably limit your choice to those people who would be most likely to call you. Already you have made a logical assessment. Never mind. Just make your choice and – this is important – *write down* the name of the person you feel will be the next to call. I suggest that you keep a large notebook specially for this purpose, to record all your guesses, impressions and predictions. Write down the date, the time and the guess or prediction. If it turns out that you are correct, write this down. If you are wrong, this also must be faithfully recorded. A typical page should look something like this:

Sat/May/23/19-- 'The next person to telephone me will be John.'
Outcome: Incorrect. The next caller was my sister Jane.

Sat/May/23/19-- 'When Sue arrives she will be wearing green.'
Outcome: Partly correct – she was wearing a green dress.

Sun/May/24/19--'The winner of 2.30 Goodwood: Happy Jack'
Outcome: Correct – Happy Jack won by two lengths.

Sun/May/24/19--'The first person I pass on the street will be a man.'
Outcome: Incorrect – the first person I passed was an old woman.

You can make guesses and predictions about almost anything: the colour of the next car that passes, the title of the next tune to be played on the radio, the name of the next caller on a radio phone-in programme – and so on. Make at least twenty such predictions every day.

It is important that you keep a full and faithful record of all your predictions and guesses, whether they are right or wrong. It is no good your saying, after the fact, 'I knew such-and-such a thing would happen.' If you do not write it down beforehand, it does not count.

These 'guessing games' will enable you to flex your psychic muscles and help to convince your deep mind that you are serious in your efforts to increase your psychic powers. And there is a powerful, positive psychology in the act of making a number of definite decisions every day.

Do not be afraid to be wrong. There is no penalty for getting it wrong. Remember, *the fear of making an incorrect assessment is part of the conditioning that you are trying to leave behind.* You should, of course, *want* your guesses and predictions to be right. Success motivation is an important factor, but the necessity to guess or predict without fear of failure is an even more important one. This fear of getting it wrong leads some professional psychics to develop the trick of phrasing their pronouncements in such a way as to be retractable if incorrect: 'I see you surrounded by flowers – have you celebrated an anniversary recently? No? Well, perhaps there's a wedding invitation coming ..'

Professional clairvoyants, who are always under strong pressure to come up with the goods, may be tempted to make vague, ambiguous statements of this kind when their powers momentarily desert them. You, however, must avoid falling into this trap. You must be *specific* in all your predictions. If you hedge your bets you will retard your development and become adept, instead, at deluding yourself and those who may seek your counsel. You must put yourself in the position of the stage mentalist who had to resort to ESP to come up with the right answer. You have got to stick your neck out and predict – or guess – with complete confidence – that such-and-such a thing will happen. You must, *at least for that moment*, play the part of the world's greatest seer. Pretend you have the ability to see into the future, and in so doing you will create the necessary psychic framework in which your powers can manifest.

Use the Mme Za Za principle to draw forth your suprasensory abilities. Do not be afraid to make public your guesses and predictions. Tell your friends what you feel is going to happen next. Put yourself on the spot. Utilize the crisis factor. Since ESP is most effective in situations of personal, emotional crisis, you have got to duplicate this type of situation; to deliberately create an *artificial crisis* in which success can only be achieved through psychic means.

Do this without a 'safety net' – which is to say, do not make vague or obscure statements, and do not make light of your predictions because you are afraid of being wrong. Of course your predictions will not always be right: even the world's greatest psychics and seers get it wrong occasionally. But your guesses will be right more and more often and, more importantly, *you will begin to know when they are right or wrong*, and you will learn to recognize the unmistakeable feeling that accompanies high-quality ESP impressions.

Exercise 2

Take a small object – something simple like a pencil or a finger ring – and place it on the floor. Kneel a few feet away from it, sitting back on your heels, and control your breathing; breathe slowly and deeply for about five minutes. Once again, the room should be warm and well-ventilated, and the lights should be dimmed.

After you have settled into a slow and steady breathing rhythm, focus your attention on the object in front of you. Begin by simply noting the details of its shape, texture and colour. Become aware of the space occupied by the object. Using your imaginary X-ray vision, see into the object; become aware of its interior. Become aware, also, of its weight and density. Do not 'concentrate' on the object, simply observe it closely; there should be no effort involved. If you find yourself knitting your brow as you focus on it, then you are trying too hard. Concentration, in the sense of making an effort, creates tension, which, as we have seen, is counterproductive in exercises like this one.

When you have familiarized yourself fully with the object and noted its every detail, close your eyes and try – again, using minimum effort – to retain the image of the object in your mind. Visualize it as though you were actually looking at it with your eyes open. Most people find this extremely difficult to do. If you cannot hold a clear image of the object, open your eyes and study it again, for perhaps half a minute. Close your eyes and try again.

Carry on in this way, opening your eyes each time you are unable to sustain the image. Do not be too quick to give up, however, and reopen your eyes only when you are sure that you cannot hold the object in your mind.

Be patient. Whilst some people may have little or no difficulty doing this exercise, others will find it next to impossible, and it may take many months of regular practice to master. When you are ready – perhaps ten or fifteen minutes after commencing the exercise – pick up the object and place it in your open palm. Cover it with the other hand. Feel the object; become conscious of how soft or hard it is; become aware of its temperature. Become sensitive to any other, more subtle vibrations emanating from it.

Try to translate your feelings about the object – even your most fleeting impressions – into metaphors: does the object convey a feeling of darkness or light? Pain or pleasure? Happiness or sadness? Friendliness or hostility? Strength or weakness? Give the object as many attributes as possible. If it could speak, what do you imagine it would say? If it was magically transformed into an animal, what animal do you think it would be? Is the object male or female?

Once again, some people will find it exceedingly difficult to glean such qualities from an 'inanimate' object – apart from its texture, temperature and so on – whilst others will experience no trouble at all with this.

If you find it difficult to go beyond the physical characteristics of the object, never mind; your ability will improve with time and practice. In the meantime, go as far as you can go in terms of colour, shape, weight, texture and the like.

To end this exercise, close your eyes for a few moments, take a deep breath, exhale, open your eyes and slowly get up.

Memory and ESP

If I describe an object to you as being round, edible, green with a reddish tinge – it shouldn't take you long to figure out that the item in question is an apple. With just a few bits of information your mind can build up a kind of 'photo-fit' image of an apple, based on your previous experience of what an apple is like. However, the apple you see in your mind's eye is not the same one that I have described; *Your* apple-image is an amalgam of every apple you have ever encountered. *My* apple-image is based on my experience of the fruit.

If you say the word *apple* to ten different people you will convey a general idea of the object, but each individual will have a slightly different image of what an apple should be. Our impressions – whether psychic or otherwise – are coloured by our past experiences of similar things. Memory plays a major part in the way we perceive the world around us, and in the way we form our impressions. The mind is lazy; it does not like to have to make fresh assessments. If the object, event or person encountered is similar in just a few respects to something or someone encountered in the past, the mind will simply unload those qualities it associates with the previous experience onto the new event. As a fairly obvious example of this mechanism, most people expect individuals who are similar in appearance to possess the same character and personality traits. We often take an instant liking – or dislike – to someone, simply because that person reminds us of someone we already know. Perception is shaped by *memory*. The qualities of most objects and events that we have to deal with are largely subjective. An apple that is sweet-tasting to one person may seem bitter to another.

Memory is particularly important with regard to *psychic perception*. Psychic impressions arrive via the memory banks. Invariably, the impression, when it filters through to the upper or conscious mind, is clothed in terms and images that are familiar to the experient. For example, a premonition of, say, a house on fire, will often have strong elements of a remembered fire. This is the answer to a question that I am often asked: 'Where, in your head, do your psychic impressions come from?'

When I demonstrate clairvoyance by telling people about things that have happened or will happen to them, I feel as if I am *remembering* these events. When a stranger comes to me for a psychic reading, I search my memory for information about him or her. And when the impressions come, it is a similar sensation to that which occurs when one's dream is 'broken'. Sometimes the 'memory' comes to me in a rush, all at once; I meet someone for the first time and in an instant I 'remember' various things that have happened to him or her. More often, however, the 'memory' is vague and fragmentary – like a dimly remembered event from the distant past, the details of which come to the surface gradually, in snatches.

Memory is the psychic route. When you want to pick up psychic impressions from people and objects, do not attempt to project your mind into the future, or you will probably end up making a logical evaluation of the situation; instead, you should behave as if the information you want was once known to you, but you have since forgotten it. Do not attempt to *acquire* this information, but try to *recall it to mind*. Do not look for visions or voices in your ear; ESP impressions rarely come this way. Be receptive, instead, to the memory process.

The Voltage of ESP

ESP operates, as we have seen, on an emotional rather than an intellectual level. Intellect plays no part in the psychic process. *Emotion* is the 'voltage' of ESP. When you want to transmit information via the psychic channels, that information must be accompanied by an emotional charge. For this reason it is generally much easier to send and receive information of a personal nature than it is to send and receive abstract or technical information. This is also why the most dramatic instances of ESP – premonitions of disaster, visions of friends or relatives who are in danger, and so on – occur in circumstances of intense personal crisis, and why it happens that, in laboratory tests into ESP, most subjects achieve higher scores at the beginning of each series of tests, their success rates declining as they lose their enthusiasm – that is, their *emotional* involvement – for the experiments.

The more emotionally charged the message is, the more likely it is to be picked up by the person to whom it is directed. It is not essential for the information itself to be of an emotional nature in order to be successfully transmitted, although such information would be easier to feel emotional about. For instance, it would be easier to transmit an image of a plane crash, than, say, the image of a piece of furniture, simply because the image of a plane crash would tend to evoke more emotion than the image of an armchair.

It is perfectly possible to convey abstract information provided that it is linked to a strong emotional charge. In other words, it is the intensity of feeling that is important, rather than the nature of the information transmitted.

Individuals with strong emotional ties – husband and wife; mother and child; brother and sister – have a much greater chance of achieving successful psychic communication, regardless of the nature of the information involved.

Mystics and witches have always been aware of this link between psychic communication and emotional intensity. In black magic, a wax doll is fashioned in the image of the intended victim, to act as a focus for the emotional intensity that the magician generates through ritual. At the moment when the doll is stabbed with a thorn or a needle, the psychic message of destruction is sent.

Hexes and curses are, in effect, psychically transmitted self-destruct commands, which are planted in the victim's deep mind and responded to at a subconscious level. The individual who is the target of such an attack may not have any inkling of what is happening; sometimes however, the victim is told about the hex, so that the command is reinforced at a psychological level, through the power of suggestion.

In absent healing the process is the same, except that the directive is a positive, rather than a negative one. In this instance, the body's self-healing mechanism is activated by the psychic command of an experienced absent healer.

The strength of a psychic impression largely depends upon the intensity of the emotion that accompanies it. This applies to all aspects of ESP – precognition, telepathy and general clairvoyance.

Unfortunately, the most powerful human emotions are usually of the negative kind – fear, pain, hate and so on. Such feelings are seldom matched, in their intensity, by the more positive emotions of tranquillity, love and pleasure. This is why most of our premonitions are concerned with tragic events like earthquakes, train crashes and similar disasters. It is the emotional impact of these events which gives them psychic 'clout'.

The most common form of telepathy occurs when the sender is in a crisis situation. For example, a mother may become aware that her child is drowning several miles away. The premonition may take the form of a full-blown vision or just a vague, persistent feeling that something is wrong. This kind of disaster-awareness less commonly involves sudden or unexpected death, such as by electrocution, because in such cases the sender is not conscious of the danger to his or her life and so does not build up an emotional charge. The majority of crisis apparitions and premonitions involve peril of which the victim is cognizant – such as drowning, live burial in landslides and so on. In these instances, victims have ample time to become sufficiently emotional about their predicament to transmit a psychic distress signal of considerable strength.

When you want to make psychic contact with another individual, you should first try to establish an *emotional* link with that person. It will do you no good at all to sit and 'concentrate' on him or her. Somehow, you have got to work up some feeling, either about the message that you wish to send, or, better still, the person whom you are aiming to reach.

To begin with, you should visualize this person as clearly as possible, and recall to mind as many personal details as you can – tone of voice, personality traits, distinctive body scent, style of dress and so on. Obviously, it will help you to have a photograph of your contactee, but failing this, you should hold an object that once belonged to him or her.

Visualize, also, the individual's present location, or, if you have no information about this, 'see' your contactee in his or her usual environment.

Contemplate these things rather than concentrate on them. If you have memories that are shared by the person you are trying to reach, run through these in your mind. Remember, ESP works through the memory banks.

If circumstances allow, speak your message aloud, exactly as you would if the person was actually standing in front of you. Again, no effort of will is required, so *do not concentrate*. You must put *feeling* into the exercise rather than mental effort.

As soon as you have sent your message, *forget about it*. This is most important. If you dwell too long upon the contents of your message, the information will be assimilated and absorbed into your own mental process, instead of being transmitted on a psychic level.

A variation of this technique is to write a letter or a note to the person you wish to communicate with, instead of speaking it aloud. Burn the note slowly as you call to mind the feelings and memories you associate with him or her.

CHAPTER NINE

BODY-MIND AND OUTER WORLD

One Organism

According to conventional psychology, the human entity essentially consists of two parts – a material body and a non-physical mind. The former is regarded as a vehicle or instrument through which the mind perceives and responds to 'the outside world'. The mind, in turn, is divided into two separate parts or functions – the conscious, or analytical mind, and the subconscious mind, which is seen as a kind of mental warehouse for the storage of past experiences, or memory and training.

The psychically aware individual perceives the human entity in a very different light. Regarded intuitively,' rather than in mechanical terms, the human psyche is recognized as a 'total mind' organism, wherein body and mind represent one integral function, rather than separate mechanisms. In this framework, the process that we call mind, though it may be focused in a specific area, is not restricted to that location but may be extended to the point of infinity. In other words, the energy field that is the body-mind does not stop at the surface of the skin but radiates, at many different levels, into the environment.

The interaction between the body-mind and the 'outside world' is far more crucial than is generally supposed. We realize that our well-being is dependent on various environmental conditions – the level of oxygen in the atmosphere, the temperature, and so on – but, when 'normal' conditions prevail, we are inclined to forget or underrate the degree to which we depend upon and *are a part of* our environment. We tend to regard ourselves as being *in* the world rather than *of* it. We perceive the world as a location in which we are based, as a reality that exists outside of us. There is little awareness or appreciation of the forces and the subtle energies of which we are a part, and to which we respond at electrical, biological and psychical levels.

According to the holistic, or body-mind view, the thing that we call conscious awareness is the point at which our intelligence is most dense, or concentrated: the place, the time and the event upon which our awareness-energy is focused. In this framework, the processes of thought and awareness can be seen as the activating of specific energy patterns within an infinite system of interacting energy fields of varying densities.

Your thoughts are not confined to your head; they are shared by the world around you, of which you are a part. At this moment, your mind – by which I mean your awareness – is focused on this page, on these words. To a lesser degree your intelligence is focused on the room that you are in; your surroundings, the noise of the traffic outside – and so on. In other words, your whereabouts is not precisely located at all, but *focused* in a particular place.

When a pebble falls into a pool of water it sends a ripple outwards in every direction. As the range increases, the strength of the wave decreases, so that it becomes difficult to detect at a certain distance.

Awareness is a similar process in reverse: it closes in to a given point, an area of maximum concentration. Most people have only a vague notion of their location in space and time. If you close your eyes right now and try to get a fix on your precise whereabouts, you will discover how difficult it is. Sight being the dominant sense for most of us, we tend to identify our location by reference to this.

Try this simple experiment. Close your eyes and think of where you were this time yesterday. See yourself there. Notice anything unusual? For example, the fact that you see yourself, in your memory, from the *outside*, as you would perceive another person, and not from 'inside your head', as you would expect if this were the true location of your awareness.

If you want to develop fully as a psychic, you must learn to identify yourself as a real and integral part of the world, and not an outside observer. You have got to relate to the forces that surround you, and be aware of the energy exchange that is constantly taking place. You must acknowledge the fact that there is a universal energy, or vital force, linking all things, and that this energy is responsive to intelligence and to emotion.

Mind and body are one. You must understand and appreciate this concept if you are to expand your mind and realize your psychic potential.

Vibrations

Everything in the universe vibrates and radiates its own particular wavelength: nothing is ever completely dead or motionless. Just as the ripples caused by a pebble falling into the waters of a vast lake expand and radiate in ever-widening circles, so even the most minute particle emits a constant stream of its own life-force.

This is not a one-way process; every object *absorbs* as well as *transmits* energy, just as its own life-force is absorbed by everything around it. Without this constant interaction of energy, life – the universe itself – could not exist. The rate at which the string of a guitar vibrates determines its wavelength and thus the musical note that reaches our ears. If two strings, whose vibratory rates are not compatible, are struck simultaneously, the resultant sound will be discordant and unpleasant to the ear. We would then say that the notes do not harmonize: they vibrate on incompatible wavelengths.

The same thing applies with regard to colours. When two colours radiate on inconsistent wavelengths, we say that they 'clash' – they do not complement each other; they are not in *harmony*.

It has been established beyond all doubt that sounds, colours and other electromagnetic vibrations can profoundly affect people, in terms of physical health and well-being, as well as psychologically. Certain colours, for example, can induce nausea and mental depression in individuals exposed to them over a long period. Other colours possess beneficial or healing properties.

Most divinatory and magical systems – and most clairvoyants – put great emphasis on vibrations, and the importance of *psychical* as well as physical harmony.

Whereas science acknowledges the existence of physical vibrations only – i.e. that only things having physical substance radiate – in psychic terms *all things* vibrate and radiate wavelengths, including abstract things like names, colours, numbers and symbols.

In science, a number is meaningless unless it represents some material quantity. In psychic terms, a number is a real thing, valid in itself, vibrating on its own particular wavelength. In science, distant events are isolated and unconnected. In psychic terms, everything relates to something else; everything connects; everything has meaning.

With the aid of a musical instrument, like a piano, it is possible to organize and manipulate sound vibrations in a controlled and meaningful way. A piano is, in effect, a system through which musical ability can be expressed. Divinatory systems like the Tarot and the I-Ching fulfil a similar function with regard to psychical ability.

CHAPTER TEN

PSYCHOMETRY

Psychometry is the ability to pick up psychic impressions by touching or holding personal objects, such as items of jewellery. When an object is carried or worn by an individual for any length of time, it absorbs some of that person's psychic energy. The trained psychometrist can pick up this energy vibration and 'see' various events and experiences connected with the object's owner. The strength of this psychic vibration can vary considerably; again, the emotional content will determine this.

In many ways the process of psychometry is similar to that of recording and playing back 'impressions' on video or magnetic tape – it could even be argued that magnetic tape recording is the technological application of psychometry. In both instances the information is energy-coded at a particular vibratory level, and playback is accomplished by attuning to the appropriate vibration and amplifying the signal. This is where the comparison ends, however. In the case of magnetic tape-recording, the energy-information is coded in a linear way, whereas psychometric information is stored in hologram form.

It may be possible, one day, to construct a psychometry machine capable of playing back the history and 'experience' of any object. The implications of such an invention would be profound. Major historical and religious events could be reviewed, and many of the world's greatest mysteries resolved.

The idea of such a machine may seem far-fetched at the moment, but I have no doubt that it will become possible in the future. In the meantime, however, we must rely upon our psychic faculties to gain access to this type of information.

An experienced psychometrist can often 'read' a personal object with a high degree of accuracy; but it is surprising how many people achieve good results after only the first or second attempt. In fact psychometry is a power that most people use all the time, without even thinking about it – for example, when you shake hands with a person and you get an instinctive feeling about them: even after the briefest contact, you may take a violent dislike to someone who had previously seemed perfectly nice. This, of course, is the most direct form of psychometry, which can also be called contact telepathy.

The instant you come into contact with an object, you begin to absorb energy from it (just as it absorbs energy from you). This energy is coded with information relating to the owner of the object. The process is a natural and automatic one; you do not have to 'try' for it. What you must do is become *sensitive* to the vibrations emanating from the object. You must become the ideal medium – that is, you have got to put yourself in the appropriate state of body and mind – to facilitate the absorption of this energy-information into the deeper layers of your consciousness. Complete physical relaxation is essential, to this end, and the absence of mental effort. So often I have seen psychometrists clutching objects tightly, with their faces screwed up in concentration – precisely the reverse of what is required for successful clairvoyance.

How to Psychometrize

1. The object should ideally be one that has been worn or carried by its owner for a period of at least one year. If the object is very old, or has been owned by a number of different people, it may be 'over saturated' and difficult to read.

   Although it is possible to get good-quality information from items made of cloth, paper, wood and other materials, I have found that gold and other precious substances give best results. I do not know why this should be so, but it is.

2. Do not touch the object until you are ready to begin to psychometrize it.

3. Before taking the object, relax consciously and take a few deep breaths.

4. Again, before you touch the object, you should remain quite motionless for a minute, breathing slowly and deeply.

5. Take the object with the fingers of both hands. Hold it lightly. It may help you to close your eyes at this point, but remember, no mental effort is required or desirable. Do not, at any time, squeeze the object.

6. Do not try to force an image or impression. Instead, try to become aware of the physical properties of the item. Feel the texture, hardness, temperature, shape and so on, of the object. Acknowledge these physical properties.

7. Gradually begin to extend your perception of the object. Follow the procedure described in exercise 2 – i.e. begin to assess the object in terms of metaphors. What taste does it impart? Is it male or female? What colour does it inspire? – and so on.

8. Take a deep breath and start talking about the object and its history. Don't worry about what to say, and don't be concerned about being right; just verbalize whatever comes into your head; and if nothing comes, keep talking. Say anything rather than nothing. Talk nonsense, but *talk*, and don't stop for at least a few minutes.

   If the object's owner is present, you can now ask him or her if your pronouncements meant anything. You can also invite questions, of a personal nature, which you must answer *without an instant's hesitation*. If the owner of the object is not present, you should write down all your impressions – or, better still, get someone else to take notes.

9. Take only one object at a time, even if the second object proffered belongs to the same person.

When you begin to psychometrize an object, the first or strongest impressions that you pick up will usually relate to the most dramatic or emotion-packed events in the object's history. And, as we have seen, such events tend to be of a negative kind – illnesses, accidents, emotional problems and so on. This means that the subject's worst qualites will tend to be emphasized in a psychometric reading, and it is all too easy to jump to the wrong conclusion that he or she is a thoroughly nasty character, constantly surrounded by negative influences and misfortunes.

You must allow for this negative bias, therefore, and bear it in mind that the information you pick up may not be at all representative of the normal lifestyle or typical routine of the object's owner.

Some substances appear to be more conducive to psychometry than others. As I have said, the more rare and expensive materials, gold, precious stones – are usually easiest to read. Objects which have been in contact with high-frequency electrical machinery are sometimes wiped clean of impressions, or 'scrambled', so that the information produced is nonsensical. This would once more indicate a connection between electrical and psychic energies.

Objects which have been left in running water – such as those that come from the bodies of drowning victims – are often devoid of significant information; which accords with the traditional magical belief that objects can be cleansed of negative psychic vibrations by immersing them in running water, and that the effect is real, not merely symbolic.

CHAPTER ELEVEN

THE PSYCHIC MENTALITY

At the beginning of this book, I emphasized the necessity of carrying out the given exercises regularly and flexing the psychic muscles at every opportunity, rather than merely reading the text in the vague hope that some kind of psychic revelation may occur. Regular exercise is as important for psychical development as it is for physical development.

To make another comparison between musical ability and the psychic faculties: it is not enough to be musical if one has not mastered a technique: it is like saying, 'If I could play the violin, I could play it brilliantly.'

The musical genius has to make himself the perfect channel through which his inspiration can be expressed. Only when his technique has been perfected can this be accomplished. The master musician-composer does not *create* music with his skill; rather, his technical ability merely enables the music to be expressed freely and with less intellectual preoccupation. It is a similar situation with ESP. The power is valuable – an asset rather than a liability – only when it is accompanied by a disciplined mind, and when an effective technique – or group of techniques – through which it can manifest, has been perfected. Along with the need for constant practice and improvement of technique, there is one other very important factor in the process of psychic development, namely the attitude of the student – not just his attitude to ESP and psychic matters, but his attitude to life in general. I have already explained how certain personality traits have come to be associated with strong ESP abilities – the most notable of these being optimism, extroversion and other outgoing qualities, and belief in the reality of psychic power.

There is a certain attitude, a way of looking at things, which promotes psychic sensitivity. It is an outlook – a 'psychic mentality' – that you must strive to cultivate if you want to fully realize your psychic potential.

Belief and ESP

If a man does not believe that he can walk, then he cannot. If a man does not believe that he can see, then he will be blind. If a man is convinced that there is a death curse on him, then he will surely die.

Belief is stronger than will-power; imagination is more powerful than mental concentration. This principle, with which all psychologists are familiar, is the basis for the phenomenon of hypnosis, and the reason why thousands of people are handicapped by 'functional' disorders – including blindness and paralysis – when there is nothing physically or mechanically wrong with them.

Before you can carry out the simplest action you must first acknowledge that it is something which is possible for you to do. With belief, incredible things are possible: without belief, nothing can be accomplished; no development can take place.

The importance of belief to ESP has been demonstrated in the laboratory many times. Test subjects who believe or accept the reality of psychical phenomena usually achieve much better results than those who have no opinion either way. And sceptics rarely, if ever, have any success in psychic experiments. A positive attitude, therefore, is crucial to ESP awareness. Only by acknowledging the reality of a phenomenon can you create the mental, emotional and psychical framework in which that phenomenon can occur.

The purpose of this book is to instruct the reader in the practical aspects of ESP development: it is presumed that he or she *believes* in the reality of the phenomenon. But it is often the case that individuals who accept one aspect of a phenomenon may reject another. For example, people who find it easy to believe in clairvoyance (perhaps because they have had direct experience of it) may find it difficult to believe in PK or mind over matter (which they are less likely to have personal experience of).

Are there ESP phenomena of which you are doubtful or sceptical? If so, I would urge you to re-examine your attitude towards them and try to make a fresh assessment based only on your direct experience of the phenomena, rather than on what you have heard or read. I am not asking you to believe just for the sake of it, or against your better judgement – only that you should not dismiss any possibility on the basis of second-hand information: keep an open mind.

In the psychic realm, where new realities are being discovered and explored, the need for a positive mental attitude is of paramount importance. If, for instance, you do not accept the possibility that there is an aura surrounding the human body, it is unlikely that you will ever be able to learn to see it. The mind, as I have said, is lazy. It will resist the introduction of anything that it regards as unacceptable, impossible or irrelevant. The thing perceived must be within the scope of the mind's framework of possibilities (it is for this reason that one or two individuals in a group of people may see a 'ghost' or other apparition, whilst the others present may not be able to see anything at all).

Some time ago my aunt bought a new television set, which she used for several weeks with no problems. Then she was visited by her 13-year-old niece. The girl complained of hearing a high-pitched whistling noise emanating from the set (no mystery about this; young ears are more sensitive to high-frequency sounds). My aunt listened, straining her ears, but could hear nothing. She asked her niece to describe the sound, which she did as best she could – but my aunt still could not detect it ... until an hour later, when she became aware of an ear-piercing whistle coming from the set. From then on she could hear the sound whenever the set was turned on. It was so unbearable, she had the set replaced within a few days.

There is nothing very remarkable about this incident, but it does serve to demonstrate the way in which the mind and the senses can be 'stretched' to take in previously unrecognized phenomena. In other words, the range of perception can be extended once the mind has become aware that there is something there to which it can extend. My aunt would never have become aware of the high-pitched sound had its existence not been conveyed to her by someone else whose sensory apparatus was sensitive enough to detect it. It is very unlikely that my aunt's hearing improved in any physical way. What happened was that her *awareness* was expanded – just a fraction, but enough to detect a reality of which she would otherwise have remained oblivious. A similar expansion of consciousness would enable many individuals to see the human magnetic aura.

In order to expand your range of awareness and perception, you must regularly exercise your powers of creative imagination. The most obvious way to do this is through pursuits such as painting, music (playing it rather than listening to it), acting, writing, dance and so on. But you can also expand your awareness by using your senses in an aggressive way. Most people are content to play a passive role and let sensations wash over them, instead of *reaching out* to touch, taste, smell, see and hear the world around them. Very few individuals actively probe the environment with their senses. In order to develop the 'psychic mentality', you must be in command of your senses, rather than a slave to them. You have got to be outgoing and responsive to everything that is happening around you. Be curious about everything. Ask questions. Expand your mind in every direction. Develop new interests. Do everything possible to keep your mind alive, responsive and in touch with its environment.

I have already explained the part played by emotion in the psychic process ('Emotion is the voltage of psychic power') – and the outgoing, optimistic personality is usually accompanied by enthusiasm, energy and a positive emotional response to the world. Nothing cuts off the psychic energy flow more effectively than emotional disorders like fear, guilt, depression, confusion and so on. The outgoing personality tends to be less neurotic and more able to express thoughts and feelings with more freedom. ESP is about keeping all channels open: the psychic and the emotional channels are, as we have seen, closely linked.

It is necessary to create, by every means available, a mental framework that will be most conducive to ESP. The mind can only operate at full power when it is properly directed, and when it regards the objective it is presented with as not only possible, but *relevant*. The mind will not assist in the development of a faculty or skill which it considers irrelevant to the everyday requirements of the individual. You must, therefore, convince your deep mind that you are serious about wanting to develop your psychic powers. It is not enough to merely acknowledge psychic impressions when they come, *you must act on them*, without hesitation and without exception. You have got to find ways of applying your ESP to everyday problems and situations, rather than to encourage psychic flashes for the momentary 'buzz' they provide.

You must learn to live instinctively. Make ESP a real part of your life. Depend upon your psychic powers to protect you and guide you clear of trouble. *The more you rely on your powers, the more they will work for you.*

The next time you lose your engagement ring or your wallet, do not despair when you cannot find it straightaway. Instead, see if you can locate it using one of the divinatory techniques given in this book. When someone offers to sell you a raffle ticket, do not accept the one proffered; instead, select one from the bunch, and trust your ESP to help you make the right choice.

When your cat or dog goes missing, get hold of a map of your area and use your pendulum to divine the place where you must begin your search.

The next time you want to get in touch with someone, do not telephone or write to them until you have first tried to get them to contact *you*, using the technique given on pages 55 and 56.

When your car develops a fault, see if you can locate the problem using psychic methods, before taking it to the garage.

Remember, ESP is a constant process, something to be elicited rather than produced. You do not need to acquire this power; all you have to do is provide the ideal conditions in which it can manifest. You must, in other words, become the perfect medium through which this power can flow.

It is not so much a matter of becoming more psychic as one of becoming less un-psychic.

Inspiration

ESP is an unconscious function. You cannot force it or will it to manifest, any more than you can will yourself to fall asleep. The process is activated when certain conditions prevail, and when the mind is sufficiently sensitive and attuned to detect subtle impressions.

This is not to say that ESP cannot be controlled; it can, but only to a limited extent. It is a similar situation to that which occurs when one sets out to paint a picture; the actual technique is under the artist's conscious control, but the creative guiding force – variously called inspiration, feeling or intuition – is not subject to this control. Technical skill alone is not enough to create a work of art: without inspiration the end product, whether it be a painting, a book or a musical composition, will be flat and lifeless. Consider how few literary experts write best-selling books. Then there are painters, master forgers, who can duplicate the great works of art to near perfection, yet whose own original paintings are mediocre. The crucial inspiration for art, cannot be forced. But, on the other hand, this inspiration is useless unless it is accompanied by technical skill.

Precisely the same thing applies with regard to ESP – which is the reason I have repeatedly made comparisons between ESP and various forms of art. It could even be argued that true art is the physical expression of psychic perception: very often art does not 'make sense' or represent physical or even psychological values. The phenomenon of artistic appreciation – why we derive pleasure from certain arrangements of sounds, shapes and colours – is as illogical and frequently as inexplicable as psychic awareness. Apart from these considerations, however, it is certainly a fact that ESP and creative expression are seldom far apart.

To develop 'pure' ESP – that is, psychic perception without the use of divinatory aids – the most important thing for you to do, in addition to carrying out the exercises given in this book, is to learn to distinguish between psychic and non-psychic impressions.

Let us go back to what happens when you begin to psycho-metrize an object. As soon as you touch it, an idea or an image may come into your mind. But how can you tell whether or not it is a psychic impression, and not just a product of your vivid imagination? Sometimes psychic 'flashes' are so vivid, and of such intensity, that there can be no mistake as to their nature; but for the most part, the impressions you receive will be so vague and fleeting as to be almost indistinguishable from the thousands of stray thoughts and ideas that come into your head every day. So how can you be sure that your impression is a psychic one, and not just a guess – or that the object reminds you of something or someone and your impression is nothing more than a mental association? How can you be certain, when you are holding the object and making pronouncements, that you are being psychic and not just lucky or clever?

The answer is, *you cannot*. All that you can hope for, in the beginning at least, is for a reasonably high percentage of your impressions to be psychically based. In other words, if you make three or four statements in the course of a psychometry reading, and ESP is responsible for just one of these, then you will be doing quite well.

What you should be aiming for, initially, is a percentage above chance. It does not matter how small this is; you will be able to improve on it later. You are aiming for a situation in which you are more likely to be right than wrong in what you say. If you carry out the advice and the exercises given in this book, your ESP will come to the fore with increasing frequency, and your 'guesses' will become more inspired. You have got to depend upon this whenever you give any kind of psychic reading – whether it be for yourself or for someone else – instead of trying to force your powers to work for you. If you have attended to the exercises and the basic training, the back-up will be there when you need it. But remember, no one is infallible: even the most gifted and experienced psychics get it wrong now and then.

CHAPTER TWELVE

DREAMS AND ESP

Because awareness is diffused during sleep, this is the time when your ESP is at an optimum. Frequently, psychic impressions will intrude on the dream mechanism and determine, or at least influence, your dream imagery. These dream impressions will be either literal or symbolic, depending on the depth of sleep.

Literal ESP dreams present no problems of interpretation: you dream of, say, a car crash, and a few days later your dream comes true in every detail. Symbolic ESP dreams, however, are not so easy to detect or interpret. Deep mind symbolism is a kind of universal short-hand language. However, there are variations of meaning from one individual to another, and some symbols have a number of possible translations. For example, if you dream of a bird it can be interpreted to signify: peace, death, a message from afar, freedom, illness and hope. The type and colour of the bird will also affect the interpretation that you make. It is also possible that the symbol refers to something that is specific to the individual, based, perhaps, on a childhood memory.

Because of these individual variations, you should not adhere too strictly to the meanings given in the index of symbols on page 73, but use it only as a very rough guide in the interpretation of your dream imagery.

You must become familiar with the language of your deep mind, and you can do this by relating this symbolism to the events of your life. This means that you will need to keep a dream diary by your bed at all times, so that when you wake up in the morning – the very instant you wake up, since dreams have a tendency to dissolve within a few minutes of waking – you can write down as many details as you can remember of what you have dreamt.

Record your dreams on the left-hand side of your dream diary. Then, every evening, before you retire to bed, you can record the events of the day on the right-hand page. In this way you will be easily able to compare your dreams with the events of the following day, and so detect subliminal ESP impressions. You will also gain a valuable insight into the workings of your deep mind and come to understand something of its symbolism. More importantly, by carrying out this dream feedback on a day-to-day basis, you will establish a closer link between upper and lower levels of mind; and as this outer-inner link is strengthened, your psychic dreams will occur more frequently.

Dream Symbolism

Aircraft:	An unexpected journey; personal risk; danger.
Angel:	Good news on the way; news from afar; inner security.
Arrow:	Troubles on the way; decisions to be made.
Baby:	Changes; minor difficulties that will be overcome.
Ball:	Uncertainty; distrust.
Box:	Inability to cope; insecurity.
Bear:	Secret fears; hidden danger; fear.
Bee:	Good news; successful outcome; material gain; changes.
Bird:	Illness; bad fortune (especially if black); hope; good news; peace; news from afar.
Blood:	Unnecessary worry; recovery.
Boat:	Need for change; material loss.
Bottle:	Health problems; treachery; danger.
Bridge:	Opportunities; need for decisive action.
Butterfly:	Relationship problems; distrust; recklessness; change.
Candle:	Guilt; concealment; insight; intelligence; hope.
Cat:	Secrecy; false friends; inner strength; magic.
Chair:	Financial gain; property deals; boredom.
Circle:	Success; achievement; completion.
Clock:	Confusion; travel; pressure; illness.
Clouds:	Need for change.

Comet:	News of a death; major change; news from afar; a visitor.
Cross:	Illness; regrets; guilt.
Dagger:	Emotional instability; danger; immaturity.
Dog:	Good news; advice needed; news of a birth; comfort.
Door:	Caution; wariness (open); frustration (closed).
Egg:	Prosperity (unbroken); fear of failure (broken).
Eye:	Idealism; need for perfection; psychic awareness.
Fire:	Anger; destruction; guilt; sexual frustration.
Fish:	Good fortune (alive); birth; fertility (dead).
Flag:	Uncertain period ahead; danger; risk.
Flower:	Ambitions achieved; need for security; yearning.
Fly:	Obsession; depression; worry; long-term problem.
Frog:	Unexpected gain; need for restraint; meetings.
Funfair:	Frustration; dissatisfaction with relationships.
Goat:	Irrational fear; sexuality; threat.
Gun:	Emotional instability; fear of failure; ill health.
Hat:	Opportunity; travel; new relationships.
Hatchet:	Mental strain; emotional frustration; fear.
Hill:	Obstacles to be overcome; ordeals.
Horse:	Romance; sexual prowess; good news; recklessness.
House:	Health problems; anger.
Island:	Self-doubt; inability to express emotions.
Jungle:	Insecurity; broken promises; temporary problems.
Key:	New friends; opportunities; danger of material loss.
Kite:	Good fortune; need for friendship; need for change.
Knife:	Instability; conflict; inability to compromise.
Ladder:	Achievement; good fortune; change.
Letter:	Financial loss; apathy; indecision.

Lion:	Concern about future; events out of control; power.
Mask:	Deception; insecurity; lack of self-confidence.
Money:	Suspended decisions; travel.
Monkey:	Ulterior motives; enemies; bad luck.
Monster:	Fear of the future; distrust.
Moon:	Secrecy; deception; uncertainty; sensuality.
Mud:	Health; good fortune; recovery.
Necklace:	Romance; self-assurance; mystery.
Oil:	Sexuality; birth; money.
Owl:	Disappointment.
Paper:	Bad news; many small worries; mental pressures; anxiety.
Parcel:	News of pregnancy or birth; a surprise; change.
Peacock:	Self doubt; minor illnesses.
Pots and Pans:	Visitors; recovery.
Puppet:	Partnership problems; guilt.
Rain:	Good news on the way; gain; new beginnings.
Rat:	Treachery and deceit; gullibility.
Rabbit:	Recklessness; overdependence on others; timidity.
Rust:	Money; gain.
Scissors:	Conflict; arguments; domestic problems.
Skeleton:	Neglect; poverty; isolation.
Snake:	Inability to express anger; frustration; secret enemies.
Spider:	Good luck; birth; determination; recovery; money.
Star:	Steady progress; intuition.
Sun:	Energy; success; optimism; good health; travel.
Tree:	Spirituality; attainment; happiness.
Water:	Need for a change; wish to escape; trouble; sensitivity.

Remember, this index is not intended to be taken too literally, and should be used only as a very rough guide in the interpretation of your dream imagery. If you keep a dream diary, you will soon become familiar with your own deep mind symbolism. Make comparisons with the meanings given here and revise where necessary. Using this list as a starting point, you can gradually compile your own, unique index of symbols and their meanings to you.

CHAPTER THIRTEEN

DIVINATION AND ESP

Most divinatory systems – including astrology, Tarot and I-Ching – are simply ritualized techniques that help us to channel and focus our innate psychic powers. Some types of divination have profound and complex philosophies attached to them, but it is not necessary to become involved in these aspects in order to take advantage of their ESP-enhancing qualities. For example you can use the Tarot to assist or complement your clairvoyant abilities without becoming steeped in ancient Tarot lore. Nor do you need to be a Romany gypsy to master the art of scrying, or crystal gazing.

It is not uncommon for ESP purists to be scathing about what they consider to be occult trappings like Tarot cards and crystal balls. And parapsychologists are usually loath to acknowledge the link between the psychic sciences and the divinatory arts.

In adopting this attitude these people reveal how little they understand about the nature of ESP. There is nothing sacred about psychic perception. It is not a possession either of science or religion; it is a natural, neutral characteristic, common to all individuals, which manifests in a variety of ways and on many different levels. More than anything else, psychic experience is a personal thing, which every individual can learn to express – like music or art – in their own way. Whether they like it or not, the parapsychologist and the crystal gazer are both involved with the same phenomenon, and both approaches are equally valid and meaningful.

ESP is something that can be improved with proper training and regular practice. If the Tarot, or some other system of divination, can help to bring this faculty to the fore, then by all means we should consider using these methods. It is possible to be musical without being able to sing: is it not permissible, them, to learn to play a musical instrument?

I myself employ various forms of divination in my psychic detection work. In one murder investigation, for instance, I used a combination of crystallomancy (crystal ball gazing), Tarot divination and straightforward clairvoyance to locate the murder suspect. When I was first consulted on the case, I used the Tarot to discover what had actually taken place (the details of the crime were not yet known); and when I visited the scene of the crime I was able, through a series of impressions, to get a clearer idea of what had happened and to confirm, for the most part, the details revealed by my Tarot reading about the event. A few days later, with the aid of a crystal ball, I was able to add a few crucial details to my earlier impressions.

By using these divinatory techniques it was possible for me to piece together different types of information in a way that would have been much more difficult using only straightforward clairvoyance.

Pendulum Dowsing

Pendulum dowsing is one of the oldest and one of the simplest methods of obtaining clairvoyant information. Although most people would associate pendulum dowsing with locating hidden underground streams and so on, in fact it is possible, with a little ingenuity, to discover a wide range of information using this technique. Pendulum divination can be used to find lost objects, to locate missing persons, to help solve problems, to diagnose illness and to prescribe treatment. It is also becoming increasingly popular in the area of diet and nutrition, where it can be used to pinpoint vitamin and mineral deficiencies, determine individual dietary requirements and to test for allergies. Specially designed dowsing pendulums can be purchased at most occult suppliers; however, it is possible to make a perfectly good pendulum with an object such as a finger ring, and a length of string or cotton.

If you have never before experimented with pendulum dowsing, the following simple experiment – which is by way of

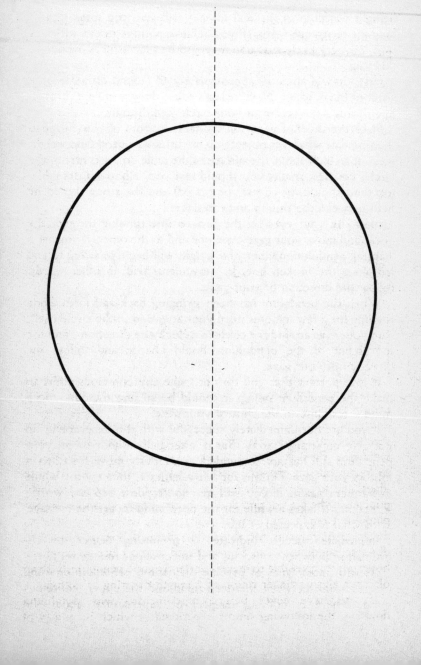

being a warm-up to the real thing – will give you some idea of how the technique works. If you achieve positive results with this test, it is very likely that you may also be successful at pendulum dowsing.

First, draw a circle of approximately 6″ (15cm) diameter on a sheet of blank paper. Next, using a ruler, draw a straight, broken line through the centre of your circle (see diagram).

Place the sheet of paper on the table in front of you. Suspend the ring – or whatever object you are using as a pendulum weight – about an inch above the surface of the table, in the centre of the circle. For best results you should rest your elbow on the table-top (you should, of course, be seated) and the string should be held between the thumb and forefinger.

Now, fix your eyes on the broken line running through the circle and move your gaze from one end to the other. If you are a 'natural' pendulum diviner, the weight will begin to swing to and fro along the broken line. Its movements will, in other words, follow the direction of your gaze.

When the pendulum has been swinging back and forth along the line for a few minutes, turn your attention to the circle itself. Run your eyes around the circle in a clockwise direction – and the movement of the pendulum should change and follow the direction of your gaze.

It is important that you do not make any conscious effort to make the pendulum swing: it should be an unconscious – deep mind – response to the shift of your gaze.

If you are not immediately successful with this experiment, do not give up straight away. But if, after half-an-hour or so, your pendulum still has not responded, consciously move it so that it follows your gaze. Do this for a few minutes, then try the whole experiment again. If you still get no response, do not worry; sometimes it takes a while for the deep mind to 'get the message' as to what is expected of it.

Immediate success indicates a promising degree of co-ordination between conscious and unconscious functions.

As with most types of psychic divination, pendulum dowsing creates a link between the deep mind and the upper, conscious mind. There is nothing magical or supernatural about the movement of the pendulum; it moves in response to minute muscular contractions, of which you are unaware. These muscular movements are directed by the deep mind in response to your questions.

The pendulum can make two basic movements. It can move in a circular motion, either clockwise or anti-clockwise, and in a straightforward left-to-right or back-and-forth motion. When the pendulum moves in a clockwise direction it generally indicates a positive or affirmative response to the question asked. An anti-clockwise motion indicates a negative response. Very often people tell me that they have tried pendulum dowsing but have been disappointed with the results they obtained. The most common complaint is that the information gleaned is often unreliable. So, the experimenter who starts off by being impressed with the pendulum – particularly when it has supplied some strikingly accurate information – loses faith in the technique when it subsequently provides a succession of incorrect answers to a series of simple questions.

For some reason, most people expect total accuracy from techniques of this kind, and when the reality falls short of this, they quickly lose interest and conclude that the method has no value. People expect psychic systems to be infallible – which, of course they are not. Again, it is a percentage above chance that you should be aiming for when you operate the pendulum; an edge that you can improve on. Remember, there is no magic inherent in the pendulum itself; it is just another method of channelling your native ESP. This is an important point to bear in mind, and one that applies equally to the I-Ching, the Tarot and other divinatory systems: the psychic information comes from *you*, and not from the pendulum – or the Tarot cards or the crystal ball. To make yet another musical analogy: an individual's musical ability remains the same, regardless of which instrument he or she plays, and, although a musician may feel more at home with a violin rather than a guitar, the use of one instrument rather than another will not improve his natural musical ability. The instrument is only as good as the person who plays it. Thus, a violinist of mediocre talent will continue to be so, even if he is given a Stradivarius to play.

Different forms of divination are like different instruments to a musician. Each one produces a different effect; each one elicits a slightly different aspect of the ESP phenomenon. But no divinatory technique is self-working: just as possession of a musical instrument does not make you musical, neither does the use of a divinatory method make you more psychic. The magic is *not* in the cards, crystal ball, pendulum – it is in the individual who employs these methods. The advantage of using these techniques is that they make it possible to exercise a certain degree of conscious control over the psychic faculty.

Method

Before using the pendulum you should always relax, control your breathing (breathe slowly and deeply – but not too deeply – through your nose) and close your eyes for a minute to still your mind and focus your thoughts on what you are doing. In fact you should carry out this little ritual before any psychic operation or exercise.

Now, ask your question, either mentally or aloud, and wait for the pendulum to respond. Do not be tempted to cause any movement deliberately. Remember, sometimes it takes a little time for the message to get through. Be patient.

Presently – and if the pendulum works for you – it will begin to swing in a circular motion. If it turns clockwise, the answer to your question is *yes*; anti-clockwise means *no*. As a warm-up, ask a few simple questions to which you know the answer. Ask questions like, 'Is my name Sarah?', or, 'Is this Friday?'

It is also a good idea, in the beginning at least, to restrict your questions to matters of a personal nature only, rather than to ask questions on world events. In general, the pendulum is more effective when it is used to deal with problems and questions of the former kind. Stick to questions about your work, your finances and your business and emotional relationships. Do not ask questions about the state of your health – not, at least, until you have become adept at handling the pendulum. Always be careful about how you phrase your questions: your deep mind – like the genie of the lamp – will usually respond to the literal meaning of your question, rather than what you really *mean*. Do not, for example, ask questions like 'Will I travel?' 'Travel' could mean a half-hour bus journey. You should also be careful to put a time limit on questions of this kind. You may get a 'yes' answer to the above question – but when will it happen? Next week? Next year? Five years from now? So, phrase your questions with care.

Always keep a record of your efforts with the pendulum. Write down the question and the pendulum's response. Never doubt the answer you get, and never 'try again' to see if you get a different response the second time (this also applies to other kinds of psychic divination). Always accept the first answer you are given. If it turns out to be wrong, then so be it; you can't be right all the time. Your success rate will improve with practice – but not if you adopt a doubtful attitude. You do not have to actually believe everything that you divine with your pendulum; you only need to *accept* the possibility that the information may be true, and to regard it as true until it is shown to be otherwise.

The main disadvantage of dowsing with the pendulum is that it is limited in the way that it can respond to questions – by giving only 'yes' and 'no' answers. The result of this is that you can easily end up by conducting a kind of 'Twenty Questions' session, which is rather tedious.

By using a little imagination, however, it is possible to overcome this problem. When you have familiarized yourself with the pendulum technique, try this experiment. On the following page is the palm print of a mystery person. Using the pendulum in the way described above, you have got to divine as many facts as possible about the subject.

Points to remember
1. For best results you should be seated at a fairly high table with your elbow rested on the surface. Pendulum string or thread should be approximately 10" in length. Make sure the weight (a heavy-ish ring) swings freely.
2. Suspend the ring about an inch above the print.
3. Formulate your question carefully and ask it either mentally or aloud. Then *wait* – don't 'urge' it to respond.
4. Record all your questions and the responses you get.

A palm print is an excellent psychic link, and it is not necessary

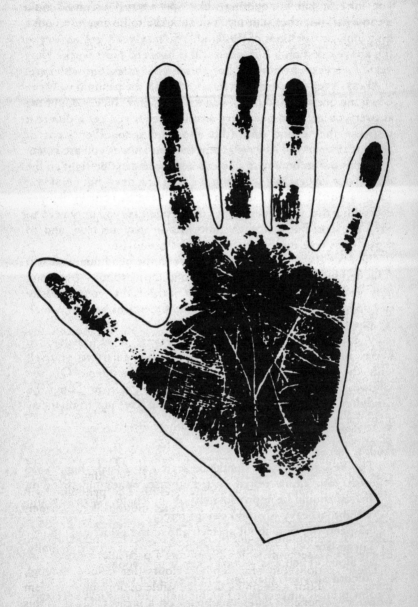

for you to know anything about palmistry. Just hold your pendulum over the palm print and ask the following questions:

Is the person dead or alive? (clockwise = alive, anti-clockwise = dead)

The mystery person was born in one of the following countries – use your pendulum to discover which one (try each one in turn):

Spain   Russia   Germany   Holland   France   Italy

The subject is or was involved in which of the following fields:
Science   Commerce   Medicine   Arts   Military

If you seem to be getting strong responses, use the pendulum to glean further information about the subject. Write down your results. Ask questions about the subject's physical appearance, character and personality traits – and so on. Do not worry if you get it wrong; it is just an exercise to familiarize you with the pendulum technique.

The identity of the subject is revealed on page 94.

The 'Pendu-scope'

As I have said, one of the main drawbacks of the pendulum is the fact that, unless you use it over a map, it can usually only give 'yes' and 'no' responses to your questions. One way to get round this is to construct a semi-circular board, as illustrated (overpage) which makes it possible to use the pendulum to select one of a dozen possible options. You could, for instance, use each division to represent a vitamin or a mineral, in order to divine your own ideal daily intake.

The pendulum should be suspended over the centre spot. In the case of dowsing for vitamins you should start by asking, 'Should I take extra vitamins to improve my health?' The pendulum will then turn in a clockwise or anti-clockwise motion. If the former, you can then go on to ask, 'Which of these vitamins do I need to take?' The pendulum should then swing to-and-fro, indicating one of the twelve sections which represents a particular vitamin.

These sections can also denote colours (for colour healing), items of food (for a slimming diet), possible options in a problem situation or possible dates to embark on a project. Used in this way, the pendulum becomes a kind of personal ouija without the trappings; an instant deep mind link-up.

Remember, although you must accept the information provided by your pendulum and act on it – at least until it is proved to be wrong – your success rate with the pendulum will reflect your general ESP level. The more you develop your psychic powers, the more accurate your pendulum divinations will become.

Pendulum Seance

It is possible, with the co-operation of several other experimenters, to conduct a 'pendulum seance', in which the pendulum responds to questions set by the group. For this experiment you will require a wire frame from which the pendulum is suspended. You can make this frame quite easily with a length of fairly soft wire such as that used to make coat hangers – or you can buy a ready-made stand at any electrical or hardware shop (some modification will probably be necessary).

Make sure that the base of the frame is firm and steady, so that the structure cannot overbalance; you can stick it to the table surface with tape or blu-tac if you wish.

The only other thing you will need for this experiment is a glass tumbler, which is placed at the base of the frame, as shown, so

that the ring or weight swings freely inside the glass, in su
position that it strikes the side of the tumbler whenever it swings
more than an inch or so in any direction. The experiment should
commence in the prescribed way, with relaxation, controlled
breathing (the group should breathe in unison) and a brief
meditation to prepare the mind. Then the experimenters should
place their hands, palms down, on top of the table, in the centre
of which the pendulum and glass tumbler have been placed.

Questions can now be asked – ideally, these should be
prearranged and well-formulated – and the pendulum will

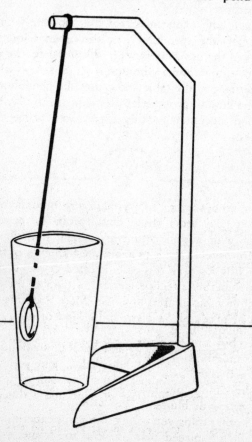

presently begin to swing to and fro until the ring strikes the side of the glass in response. If it strikes once, the answer is in the affirmative; twice indicates a negative response (this is the most common system; you can, of course, devise your own. Just make sure that all the experimenters are in agreement on the code used.) If results are slow in coming, do not despair. Once the pendulum begins to respond, there will be no stopping it, and subsequent pendulum seances with the same experimenters will tend to produce more immediate results; if the sessions are regular, it is usually possible to pick up where you left off on the previous occasion.

Once again, the explanation for the apparently supernatural movement of the pendulum is the unconscious muscular movements of the experimenters; in this instance, the response is in a collective form, and a vibration is set in motion which passes along the surface of the table and causes the pendulum to move. Very often a kind of group telepathy comes into play during this process, and occasionally this experiment brings forth true psychokinesis.

Scrying

The ancient art of scrying, or crystal gazing, is not favoured much by psychics and seers these days, probably because of its associations with gypsy fortune-tellers and fraudulent mystics. The modern psychic tends to avoid the trappings of the fortune-teller, which is a pity in this case, because crystal divination is a simple and superbly effective method of tapping the deep mind, from which psychic impressions arise. More than this, the crystal has a special magic all its own, and a kind of purity that other divinatory techniques lack.

Whereas palmistry, astrology and Tarot divination all require a certain amount of technical knowledge, and some ability to interpret and analyse symbols, the crystal ball requires nothing more than the appropriate state of mind and a reasonably high level of ESP.

Crystal imagery, like dream imagery, can be either literal or symbolic. In the latter case a certain amount of translation is required (the symbols of the crystal ball are the same as those of dreams, and have identical interpretations). More often, however, the images perceived in the crystal are straightforward representations of past, present or future events.

Although crystal gazing is the least complex of all techniques, it is also the one that people have most difficulty in mastering. This is perhaps because successful scrying requires a certain attitude of mind that is very difficult to convey to someone who has never experienced anything like it. All that can be said is that this attitude is accompanied by a sense of mental detachment that is more a reverie than a trance. If you have ever seen pictures as you gazed absently into the dying embers of a fire you will be familiar with the sensation.

The crystal ball itself does not possess any inherent psychic power. It is merely a focal point for the mind; a 'black hole' into which the imagery of the deep mind is drawn.

Method

Crystal-gazing requires that you remain immobile for up to an hour, so make sure that you are going to be comfortable before you start. The room should be warm, the lights dimmed. A blue light will promote the appropriate frame of mind. Remember to take your telephone receiver off the hook so that you are not disturbed.

Sit in a hard-backed chair with good support, with your crystal ball in front of you on a fairly high table. You can then rest your elbows on the surface as you gaze (you may use a cushion for your elbows if you wish).

The crystal should be about 10–12 inches (28 cm) from your eyes, and you should be looking down on it at a slight angle. The crystal itself should rest on a matt black cloth, to prevent unwanted reflections. Velvet is usually used for this purpose. Now you have to find the 'blob'. This is a patch of dark blue which appears when the crystal is looked at from a certain angle. The blob is much easier to find – it usually appears at the base of the crystal – than it is to describe; you will recognize it when you see it (if you cannot locate it, try changing the light source).

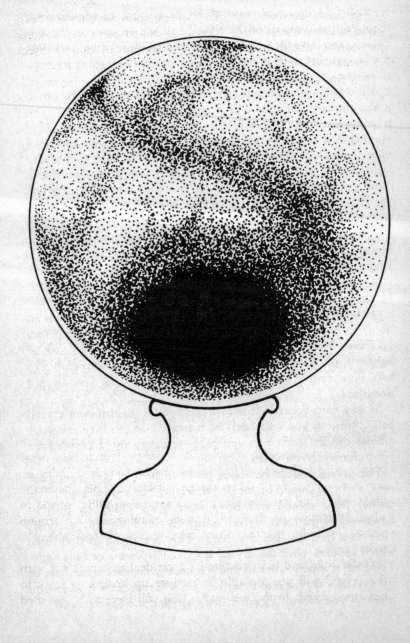

The 'blob' becomes the mind screen upon which your deep mind imagery is projected. There is, I should point out, nothing paranormal about this blob – it is merely an optical effect characteristic of all crystal spheres.

When you have found this dark blue screen inside your crystal, gaze – do not stare – into it, and wait. You must be very patient. Think of this as an exercise in mind control, so that you will not be disappointed if nothing happens for the first few times.

One of my students described her first successful scrying experience as follows:

> For perhaps forty-five minutes nothing at all happened, and I was becoming quite bored and restless with the exercise. On several occasions I became aware that my thoughts had wandered and I had to consciously drag my mind back to what I was doing. This was my fifteenth attempt at scrying; I had performed the same exercise every evening for two weeks and nothing at all had happened for me. I was ready to give up when, quite suddenly, the 'fog' cleared and I found myself gazing in fascination at a tiny 'TV screen' on which a series of images – people, buildings, outdoor scenes – came to life. Each scene lasted only a few seconds, faded, and was replaced with a new image. The detail and clarity astounded me, as did the contrast between each scene and the next. There didn't seem to be any connection between them, which somehow made it seem all the more eerie. There must have been about a hundred scenes in all ... the procession lasted five or six minutes, then finally the images just faded away completely, and that was that. I tried for a further half hour to bring them back, but with no success.

Note that this student did not see anything of any real significance in this first successful attempt at scrying. The images were random and meaningless. There was nothing familiar in them; no scenes or events she could recognize or relate to. This is often the case with first-time crystal gazing. There is an initial period in which the basic mechanism becomes established – a warm-up phase. Gradually, the images perceived become recognizable, the faces familiar.

Only when you have acquired a great deal of experience with the crystal will you be able to conjure up images in reply to questions asked. In the meantime, you will have to be satisfied with what you get: for the most part you will see little of any significance in your crystal; every now and then, however, you will see a distant or future event that you can identify and relate to.

A word of warning is appropriate at this point. Whilst it takes most people at least two or three weeks – sometimes much longer – of practice before they can see anything in the crystal, others possess a natural aptitude for this technique, and it is not unusual for such individuals to see pictures in their first scrying efforts. The experience of seeing vague shapes suddenly focus into moving images of people, places and events can be a frightening one, especially when the gazer is not really expecting anything to happen. When they come, the images possess an almost hypnotic quality in the way they take shape.

Never scry for longer than an hour at a time.

If you do not possess a crystal ball and would like to test your abilities as a scryer before you decide to go to the expense of buying one – crystals can be quite costly – you can experiment with a glass of inky water. Simply fill a tumbler to the brim with water, add a few drops of blue ink and you are ready to scry. The procedure is the same as that described for crystal gazing, but in this case there is no 'blob' for you to use as a mind screen. Instead, you must regard the surface as your projection area.

Although the crystal ball itself possesses no innate power, it is nevertheless true that best results are to be obtained from one that has been in your possession for a long period. The crystal becomes attuned to the psyche of its owner and responds to his or her personal vibration.

Most clairvoyants handle their crystal with great care, even reverence, and most would never dream of allowing another person to use it.

Quartz crystal, in particular, is an excellent medium for psychometric impressions, so that care must be taken to ensure that it is not subject to contamination. For the same reason, the ball is traditionally wrapped carefully in its cloth when it is not in use, and locked away in a safe, special place.

CHAPTER FOURTEEN

HOW TO ASSESS YOUR PROGRESS

If you carry out the exercises and follow the advice given in this book, it should not be long before your latent psychic abilities come to the fore. As I have already indicated, individuals differ in the rate at which they develop, but you can reasonably expect to see signs of progress within two to three months.

In the early stages of development your psychic impressions are likely to be subtle and fleeting rather than dramatic or intense, and this phase is usually characterized by phenomena of the kind described in the introduction to this book — flashes of intuition, feelings of *déja vu* and unusually vivid dreams with precognitive elements. (Most people are amazed to discover how often their dreams relate to future events.)

There are various simple experiments that you can carry out to test your ESP. For instance, you can have someone draw a picture of an object or a scene which you can then try to identify by straightforward clairvoyance or by using some form of psychic divination, such as crystal gazing. And you can easily test your pendulum dowsing abilities by having someone hide a small object for you to locate using the technique described on pages 80 and 81.

Now that you know the basic principles of ESP, you should have no problem devising your own tests and experiments.

If you keep a written record of your psychic experiences — including a 'dream diary' — as I have suggested, you will soon be able to recognize the physical and emotional states most conducive to ESP and learn to reproduce them deliberately. A written record also makes it easy to determine your rate of development.

*   *   *

The palm print on page 84 is that of Mata Hari, the Dutch born dancer who became a spy. Her real name was Gertrud Zelle (later Lady Cresta Macleod). Did you get it right?

INDEX